The Concrete Reserve

Corporate Programs for Indians in the Urban Work Place

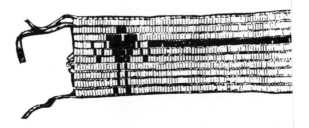

The Concrete Reserve

Corporate Programs for Indians in the Urban Work Place

Gail Grant

The Institute for Research on Public Policy

L'Institut de recherches politiques

Printed in Canada

Legal Deposit Fourth Quarter
Bibliothèque nationale du Québec

Photo: Gros d'Aillon
Cover Design: Hackett Boyer

Canadian Cataloguing in Publication Data

Grant, Gail 1943 –
 The concrete reserve

Bibliography: p.
ISBN 0-920380-93-X

1. Indians of North America--Prairie Provinces-- Employment. I. Institute for Research on Public Policy. II. Title.

E78.P7G72 1983   331.6'9'9709712   C83-090132-9

The Institute for Research on Public Policy/L'Institut
de recherches politiques
2149 Mackay Street, Montreal, Quebec H3G 2J2

To
Olivier Grant-Akian

The expression 'people of Indian ancestry' frequently used in this study is meant to include anyone who defines himself or herself in terms of the various categories of Native people (status Indian, non-status Indian or Métis) or is so defined by others in the community. The expression is inclusive, yet it allows the introduction of distinctions among different categories of people of Indian ancestry whenever it is relevant to do so.

Contents

Contents

Members of the Institute

Institute Management

Publications Available

Tables

Foreword

In the last twenty years people of Indian ancestry have migrated to cities in Western Canada in increasing numbers. For the most part, they have moved in the hope of achieving a better life than they had or thought they could find on reservations or in the villages or rural areas where they have normally lived. In many cases the result has been disillusioning. Appropriate employment opportunities have been far fewer than the number of Native people seeking jobs. This, as well as unpreparedness for new and unfamiliar circumstances, has made it difficult for them to adapt to the urban environment. The complex of problems has frequently led to reactions among the non-Indian population that have created tensions and made difficult situations worse. There is no quick or easy solution. However, it is apparent that an essential element of any program to meet the problem must be the overcoming of the difficulty that Indian people find in securing, and succeeding in, paid continuing employment. It was in recognition of this fact that the Institute, with the financial support of the Donner Canadian Foundation, undertook a study of employment programs for Native people that have been instituted by a number of companies in Western Canada.

The study by Gail Grant evolved from some suggestions for research by The Institute in 1978 entitled "Urban Institutions and People of Indian Ancestry". During interviews with government, business, and Native leaders in the Western provinces in the late 1970s, it became evident that people of Indian Ancestry who try to integrate into the urban labour market face unanticipated barriers or constraints that prevent them from obtaining or keeping desirable employment. The need for special measures had been recognized in some instances, and employment programs to attract Native candidates and to help them to adjust to the unfamiliar world of offices or plants were already operating in some firms. However, these programs were proportionately few, and there did not seem to be wide awareness of them or of what had been learned from their application.

The objectives of this study were three-fold: to identify corporate policies and employment programs aimed at the accommodation of people of Indian ancestry; to examine the characteristics of the programs, their objectives, their nature and their processes of implementation; and to identify emerging trends and changing attitudes relating to the employment of Native people. As Gail Grant states, the basic purpose was to "demonstrate the types of organizational arrangements that are conducive to the realization of a successful Native-employment program". The twenty-six suggestions set out in her concluding chapter are designed to help employers, managers and others concerned about the employment of Indian people in urban situations. The Institute hopes that this publication may encourage firms that can institute Native-employment programs, but that have not yet done so, to recognize the importance of careful planning if such employment is to succeed, but also to recognize that there may be significant advantage to the firms if such programs can be set up. Although this report is mainly directed towards employers, we hope that it may also be of interest — and encouragement — to Indian organizations and to Indian people in the cities of the West.

Gordon Robertson
President

September, 1983.

Avant-propos

Depuis les vingt dernières années, le nombre d'Amérindiens qui s'installent dans les centres urbains de l'Ouest canadien s'accroît de plus en plus. La plupart d'entre eux quittent leurs réserves, leurs villages ou leurs cadres ruraux dans l'espoir de trouver une qualité de vie supérieure à celle qu'ils connaissent. Pourtant cette migration est souvent désillusionnante. Le nombre d'opportunités d'emploi est sérieusement inférieur au nombre de postulants amérindiens. Ce fait, ainsi que le manque de préparation à des circonstances nouvelles et inattendues, rend l'adaptation à un milieu urbain très pénible. Ces difficultés ont souvent amené les populations non-amérindiennes à réagir et les tensions sociales qui en découlent n'ont servi qu'à aggraver une situation déjà précaire. Il n'existe pas de solutions rapides ou faciles. Il est cependant évident qu'un aspect critique de tout programme visant une solution est celui de surmonter la difficulté que les Amérindiens éprouvent à obtenir et à garder des emplois permanents et bien rémunérés. Convaincu de l'importance de ce facteur, l'Institut, avec l'appui financier de la Donner Canadian Foundation, a entrepris une étude des programmes d'emploi mis sur pied par un bon nombre d'entreprises dans l'Ouest canadien à l'intention des Amérindiens.

L'étude de Gail Grant représente la mise en vigueur d'une des suggestions de recherche proposées sur la question de l'Amérindien urbain dans un rapport publié par l'Institut en 1978 intitulé " Urban Institutions and People of Indian Ancestry ".

Au cours de rencontres avec des représentants des gouvernements, du monde des affaires et des associations amérindiennes dans les provinces de l'Ouest vers la fin des années 70, nos chercheurs ont constaté que lorsque les Amérindiens tentent de s'intégrer au marché du travail urbain, ils font face à des obstacles ou à des contraintes imprévus qui les empêchent d'obtenir ou de garder un emploi convenable. Certains ont reconnu la nécessité de remédier à la situation et quelques entreprises ont déjà mis sur pied des programmes d'emploi afin d'intéresser des candidats amérindiens et de les aider à s'adapter à un environnement inconnu de bureaux ou d'usines. Ces programmes sont toutefois l'exception plutôt que la règle et très peu de gens semblent être au courant de leur existence ou de ce que l'on peut retenir de leur mise en vigueur.

Cette étude vise trois objectifs: cerner les politiques et les programmes d'emploi mis en vigueur dans les entreprises dont l'objet est d'embaucher les Amérindiens; examiner les caractéristiques de ces programmes, leurs objectifs, leur nature et leurs processus d'implantation; et identifier les tendances nouvelles et les changements d'attitudes vis-à-vis la place des Amérindiens dans la population active. Comme le dit Gail Grant, l'objet principal de son étude est " de démontrer les différentes formules organisationnelles qui permettent l'implantation efficace d'un programme d'emploi visant la population amérindienne". Les vingt-six suggestions relevées au dernier chapître sont offertes dans le but de faciliter la tâche aux employeurs, aux gestionnaires et à tous ceux et celles qui s'intéressent à la question de la stabilité d'emploi des

Amérindiens dans des milieux urbains. L'Institut espère que cette publication incitera les entreprises qui ont les moyens d'implanter des programmes d'emploi à l'intention des Amérindiens, mais qui ne l'ont pas encore fait, à prendre conscience de l'importance d'une planification rigoureuse si un tel programme doit réussir et à reconnaître qu'elles aussi peuvent en bénéficier. Bien que ce rapport concerne surtout les employeurs, nous espérons qu'il intéressera, et encouragera, les associations amérindiennes et le peuple amérindien qui font partie de la mosaïque des centres urbains de l'Ouest canadien.

Gordon Robertson
Président

Septembre 1983

The Author

Gail Grant was born in Montreal and educated in French schools of the Congregation of Notre-Dame. She is a graduate of Concordia University. She began her career in the private sector and subsequently worked for the Canadian Council of Resource and Environment Ministers, where she was co-ordinator of a national committee on northern development. For the last decade, Ms. Grant has been employed by the Institute for Research on Public Policy, where she has had the unique opportunity of combining her training as a sociologist with her interest in policy matters pertaining to Canada's ethnic and cultural diversity. At the Institute, she co-authored *Urban Institutions and People of Indian Ancestry* and *La langue de travail au Québec*. For the last two years, Ms. Grant has been a member of the Executive Committee of the Montreal Career Women's Network Inc.

Acknowledgements

This project was largely funded by the Donner Canadian Foundation, and I wish to thank them, not only for a most generous contribution, but also for their encouragement throughout the entire course of this study.

Since this project focused on human resources, it obviously would have been impossible to carry out without the collaboration and wisdom of numerous individuals. I am grateful to the sixty respondents who granted me extensive, informative and thought-provoking interviews: their openness and positive attitude made this endeavour enriching and stimulating. I am pleased to single out those who granted me access to their personnel and, in some instances, even to their company records and files, and who received me with the warmest hospitality. I am referring to Frank J. Pearson, F.H. (Bert) Suter and Jessie Bulloch of the Manitoba Telephone System (MTS); C.F. Hews, W.T. Lineker, Cy Hennessy and Lawrence Weenusk of the Manitoba Division of Inco Metals Company; Maxine Geller of Manitoba New Careers; Henry Cook and Mona Wallace of the Manitoba Department of Labour and Manpower; Fred R. Bates and Donald J. Ash of the Saskatchewan Power Corporation; Lloyd Thompson and Jack Poole of Native Metal Industries; Herb A. Callihoe, Alex Gordon, John Scullion and Maryella Sneddon of Syncrude; Clive Chalkley, Ronald

T. Scrimshaw (Alaska Project Division) and Stan Sommerville of NOVA, an
Alberta Corporation; C.J. Newfeld of Canadian Cellulose Company
Limited; Bruce N. Sider of Westcoast Transmission Company Limited;
Glenn D. Matheson of Weyerhaeuser Canada Limited; B.E.A. Yeo, A.
Wilson, and E. Tiefenbach of IPSCO (Interprovincial Steel and Pipe
Corporation Ltd.); Ian W. Sinclair of the Saskatchewan Department of
Industry and Commerce; Tom Ward of Redi-Mix Company Limited; Dennis
O'Callahan of the Department of Indian Affairs and Northern
Development in Regina; and John Barr of the Saskatchewan Credit Union
Central.

For their assistance in arranging for me to fly to sites in northern
Manitoba, I am particularly grateful to G.D. Temple, Cec McIntosh and
Barry Stanhope. My special thanks also go to Harry D. Hayward, who flew
to Winnipeg for our interview, as well as to Roger Whittington and Harold
Warne of MTS; Bill Loftus, Don Sinclair and Gerry Argue of SPC; Barbara
L. Tate of NOVA; all of these people went out of their way to
accommodate me. George Robertson and Doug Deschamps of INCO
Metals, Jim Spence and John Monias of MTS, Jos and Art Kaswatum of
NMI and Randy Bear, Brian Melville Piney and George Pyne represent the
purpose of this study, and I am grateful to them for convincing me that
Native employment programs can and do work.

I was fortunate that some very special persons agreed to read my
lengthy first draft and offered me constructive criticism which I believe
has improved the final version. I include Raymond Breton, Gerry G.
Gummersell, Janet Hatfield, Guy LeCavalier, Richard Price, Ken Svenson,
and Eldon Thompson. I appreciate the time that Gordon Robertson took
to read the second draft and, more particularly, his comments, which
helped me to breeze through the final wrap-up. I wish to thank George
Calliou of Petro-Canada, who acted as one of the external referees.

I am particularly indebted to three individuals whose moral support
helped me through the difficult stages of this project: Catherine

MacKinnon, Senior Programme Officer of the Donner Canadian Foundation, Gerry G. Gummersell, Corporate and Government Liaison Officer, Office of the Rector, Concordia University and Co-Chairman of the Steering Committee, the Corporate/Higher Education Forum, and Paul Horner, who made a significant contribution at the conceptualization and questionnaire-design stages. It was a pleasure to work on the final manuscript with Jo File, the Institute's Senior Editor. Every author should have the benefit of her knowledge and love of the English language. I thank Grace Muldoon for her patience in typing the numerous versions of the text and Louise Beaudet for coping with a temperamental word-processor throughout the final stages of production.

Summary

The urban Indian is a relatively recent social phenomenon in Canada. The migration of Native people to Western cities had its greatest impact in the late 1960s and early 1970s, and one can say in the 1980s that this development is here to stay. Canadians of Indian ancestry have been migrating back and forth between reserves and cities for almost a generation, but difficult conditions in both environments prevent many of them from enjoying social and economic stability in either situation. To maintain basic survival, they are compelled to straddle two societies, sometimes fearing that they no longer fit comfortably in their home communities and believing it impossible to gain acceptance in an urban setting.

It is difficult to pin-point the precise catalyst of the early migratory movement, since there seemed to be as many 'push' as 'pull' causes. Diminishing employment opportunities on many reserves, with the resulting inactivity and boredom, created many social tensions among young people, and the city seemed to offer an escape. Futhermore, improvements in communications and transportation gave Native people more frequent glimpses of what appeared to be a better life: the bright lights and excitement of the city seem to have lured many of them away from difficult conditions that, in many instances, bordered on poverty. On the other hand, governments were then more prosperous and therefore at liberty to base many of their policies on social issues. The creation of programs and policies that would lead to equality of opportunity, just and fair treatment of ethnic minorities, a more active social conscience, and the initiation of affirmative action was on the agenda of most governments. This wave of liberalism resulted in considerable attention being paid to people of Indian ancestry. The underlying philosophy of the new Native policies was that Canadians must undo the errors of their forefathers and find ways to increase the participation of Native people in mainstream Canadian society. Governments initiated all sorts of employment and training programs, and slowly they began to influence, if not to pressure, the corporate sector to do the same.

Because unemployment had not, in the early 1970s, reached the unmanageable proportions that it has today, resistance to this pressure was not as great as it might have been in times of economic restraint. Moreover, leaders in the private sector were becoming sensitized to the spirit of the times and very much aware that they had a role to play in ensuring that corporate responsibility meant something more than devising strategies to bring in more dollars. Personnel managers became human resource managers, and as Canadians approached the 1980s, public relations departments were overshadowed by public affairs departments. Workers or employees were elevated to the category of a human resource. Against this backdrop, a number of Native-employment programs were created.

In this study, we examined a sample of employment programs launched in the last decade by the corporate sector for the purpose of attracting people of Indian ancestry to the Canadian labour market. We restricted our field-work to cities in Western Canada because Native people form a larger segment of their populations, and because there we were able to identify a comparatively large number of companies that had established Native-employment programs. We believed that the lessons to be learned from the investigation of the ten selected case-studies could be applied generally across Canada. We selected case-studies that, in our view, reflected the widest range of existing programs operating in the widest range of corporate circumstances.

The study begins by defining the term 'urban Indian' and introduces the objectives of the study. The major objective is to give visibility to the types of existing employment programs that are successful in attracting and retaining employees of Indian ancestry. It presents the rationale for this study, the methodology used to carry it out, and the general characteristics of the ten firms selected as case-studies. Secondary objectives are to highlight trends in Native employment practices and to provide models for firms that may have all the components in hand to develop similar programs, but have not yet done so. The following six chapters represent the findings in only six of the ten firms that were studied; material gathered in the other four was insufficient to justify separate chapters. It should be noted that programs in these four firms were in preliminary stages either of design or of implementation.

The Headstart Employment Corporation, a non-profit organization, was set up by the Saskatchewan Power Corporation to offer pre-apprenticeship training, academic upgrading and, eventually, full employment to potential employees who lack certain educational qualifications, and who are of Indian ancestry, or who are faced with some particular social handicap. Half of Headstart's recruits are Native persons, and half are non-Native. This program was created in 1978 and has been expanding steadily ever since. It owes most of its success to several factors: management strongly supports its activities and lends it Saskatchewan Power Corporation's financial and human resources when required; the Headstart co-ordinator had previous experience in working with Native people in Saskatchewan and is a trained social worker; recruitment takes place all over Saskatchewan, and trainees stand a fairly good chance of working close to their home communities; a vocational school in Saskatchewan is represented on the Headstart Board of Directors; and the ratio of staff to trainees is one to two. It should be pointed out, however, that because there is a strong desire for Headstart to succeed, undesirable applicants are weeded out during the screening process. Headstart looks for candidates who can demonstrate that they have already adjusted to the dominant society.

Native Metal Industries (NMI) was created in 1970 at the instigation of the president of the Interprovincial Steel and Pipe Corporation (IPSCO), who believed that Native people could use raw materials provided by IPSCO to operate a business that would salvage scrap-iron. The Governments of Saskatchewan and Canada supplied start-up funds, and the Saskatchewan Economic Development Corporation provided a parcel of land. Native Metal Industries can be considered a sheltered workshop designed solely for people of Indian ancestry who have not previously worked in an industrial setting and who are interested in being trained as welders. In the first half of the 1970s, the company was run entirely by Native people, but internal battles between members of the two Native organizations that provided its work-force at the time, as well as lack of managerial training, brought the company to the edge of bankruptcy. In 1976 a non-Native manager was hired to revise administrative procedures and discharge accumulated bad debts; further government funds were injected, employees became unionized, and a board of directors was elected.

Theoretically, NMI is Native-owned, since its shareholders are its employees, but the company is actually controlled by a board of directors, four of whom are non-Native. The directors make all financial decisions, and profits, if any, must be reinvested in the company. The assumption on which NMI was created is that Indians should be more effective than non-Indians in running an Indian business. Experience has shown, however, that good will cannot compensate for insufficient managerial expertise.

Syncrude Canada Limited has had Native employees on its staff since its incorporation in 1972, but it was not until 1978 that it formally established its Department of Native Development. The first mandate of this department was to draw up a five-year plan outlining the services and programs it would initiate to accommodate Native employees and the Native entrepreneurs operating in the communities where the company is active.

The services and programs offered by the Department of Native Development were initiated as needs were identified by its almost entirely Native staff. Many programs are designed to fill educational gaps among members of the community or employees of the company. This provision of information is based on the company's belief that education is the great equalizer, and that it must start in the community. Therefore Syncrude attempts through many of its programs to reach out to young people and communicate to them the value of education. Syncrude's programs also stress the importance of the need for change of attitudes in both Natives and non-Natives so that they can work together successfully in the same environment. Cultural awareness seminars were designed to promote this purpose.

Syncrude owes its success in the area of Native programs to many factors. The following are among the more significant: its first president's commitment to Native people; the request of its management that a senior Native employee analyse similar programs set up elsewhere in Canada and in the U.S.A. (This work culminated in an Action Plan that recommended the development of life-skills, family-counselling, and social and cultural training programs.); the signing of the Indian Opportunities Agreement in 1976 by the Indian Association of Alberta, the federal government, and Syncrude; and finally, the fact that the Department of Native Development is run almost entirely by people of Indian ancestry. To our knowledge, Syncrude offers the most comprehensive package of programs and services to Native people that is available anywhere in Canada.

The driving force behind the commitment of NOVA, an Alberta Corporation, to the employment of Native people has been its president who, since 1973, has actively tried to increase Native participation in all facets of the company's operations. Initially NOVA focused on acquiring a quota of Native employees that would reflect their percentage in the population of Alberta. When the company achieved this goal in 1980, however, it seemed somewhat artificial to focus simply on numbers. Where once the company believed that Native people formed a local resource that it was morally responsible to employ, it now recognizes that Native people are desirable employees because of their competence. NOVA's success can also be attributed to other important factors: since the launching of NOVA's Native Recruitment Program in 1976, a Native person has always been on staff to liaise with Native communities and to assist Native employees; the Opportunity Measures Plan, which was intended to guide the implementation of the Alberta section of the Alaska Highway Gas Pipeline Project, was designed by a Native person; the Northern Pipeline Agency specified conditions to be adhered to for the purpose of improving the socio-economic status of Native people in Alberta; the Alberta Vocational Centre, located at Grouard, collaborated by offering life-skills and training courses in a variety of trades; NOVA absorbed into its work-force the Native trainees who had been expected to work on pipeline construction; NOVA recognized the importance of training managers and supervisors who would be directly responsible for Native trainees.

Since NOVA does not want to produce failures, it is selective in its recruitment procedures. Preference is given to candidates who have a background of steady employment. Educational requirements are not stressed, but candidates who display the potential for getting a job done are the first to be selected. NOVA also tries to match skills with people and places individuals with similar skills in similar jobs. This strategy had the advantage of reducing opportunities for friction between Native and non-Native employees.

The Manitoba Telephone System (MTS) set up two programs whereby Native people would have access to employment opportunities. The first,

Equal Employment Opportunities (EEO), an Affirmative Action program, has been operating since 1975; the other, New Careers, was an initiative of the Manitoba Department of Labour and Manpower and operated at MTS for two years, that is, in 1976 and 1977. The EEO program was intended to increase the number of women, handicapped persons, and Native people employed by MTS in order to reflect more adequately their percentages in the population of Manitoba. The EEO consisted of a five-year plan of action and included the following steps: the identification and removal of barriers to employment; the design of specialized training programs; the retraining of interviewers and supervisors; the assessment and rewriting of company literature to remove biases and stereotyping; and the wide publicizing of the EEO policy.

New Careers is an on-the-job training and educational upgrading program based on two premises: that adults have a right to employment, and that poverty is not the result of inherent personal weaknesses, but of economic, social or geographic barriers that lock a great many individuals out of mainstream society. The *modus operandi* of a New Careers program is to restructure job descriptions and to train people only in those areas that are essential to the performance of a job, without lowering working standards. The New Careers program at MTS had strong support from management and involved a Native supervisor from the start. It had been temporarily discontinued because of government cut-backs, but discussions were continuing on ways to improve such a program if it were reinstated.

The Manitoba Division of INCO Metals Company has been hiring Native people since 1960. It was not until 1972, however, that INCO instituted a Northern Employment Program to utilize in its Thompson operation manpower located close to that northern Manitoba community by recruiting, employing, training, and retraining residents of the area. INCO's program is basically a recruitment and relocation operation run by a Native co-ordinator. INCO has not developed specialized programs for its Native employees, but it does refer those requiring assistance to appropriate agencies in Thompson. Its policy is based on the belief that self-help leads to self-development. When recruiting in Native communities, the INCO Native co-ordinator works in collaboration with a Native relocation officer of the Manitoba Department of Labour and Manpower; these two men facilitate the transition of Native employees from the home community to the urban setting. INCO expects its applicants to undergo some form of industrial training, and Native people, once hired, do not receive preferential treatment, since they are presumed to have the same work experience as other employees. After one year of service, INCO employees, whether Native or non-Native, have access to apprenticeship training at the Keewatin Community College.

Chapter 8 presents twenty-six points that, in the opinion of the researcher, merit the consideration of those involved in any aspect of Native-employment programs. These suggestions were made on the basis of an analysis of the functioning of each firm studied. Some reflect practices in use, and others represent glaring gaps in program design. Together they comprise a pooling of all the innovative and significant elements that have been built into the 'successful' programs. An encouraging number of positive steps have been taken in this field, and it is hoped that the dissemination of this information to a wide audience may contribute to more and better program planning.

Abrégé

L'Amérindien urbain est un phénomène social relativement récent au Canada. Le mouvement migratoire des Amérindiens vers les villes de l'ouest a subi la plus forte poussée entre la fin des années soixante et le début des années soixante-dix et se stabilise dans les années quatre-vingts. Les Canadiens d'origine amérindienne se déplacent entre les réserves et les villes depuis près d'une génération; cependant, des conditions pénibles dans les deux environnements empêchent plusieurs d'entre eux de jouir d'une stabilité socio-économique, aussi bien dans une situation que dans l'autre. Afin de maintenir le niveau de survie minimum, ils doivent chevaucher deux sociétés, se sentant d'une part étrangers dans leurs communautés d'origine et d'autre part rejetés par le milieu urbain.

Il est difficile de préciser la cause exacte du premier mouvement migratoire puisqu'il semble y avoir eu autant d'incitations à quitter les réserves que de motivations à s'installer dans les villes. La baisse d'opportunités d'emploi sur les réserves, aggravée par l'inactivité et l'ennui qui en résultent, crée des tensions sociales parmi les jeunes et la ville est, par conséquent, perçue comme un échappatoire. D'ailleurs les progrès réalisés au plan des moyens de communication et de transport ont permis aux Amérindiens d'entrevoir la possibilité d'une vie meilleure : l'attrait des sons et lumières des grandes villes semblaient permettre à plusieurs d'entre eux d'oublier des conditions pénibles qui bien souvent avoisinaient la pauvreté. D'autre part, les gouvernements étaient plus prospères à cette époque et plus disposés à créer des politiques portant sur des questions sociales. La création de programmes et de politiques pouvant assurer l'égalité des chances, le traitement juste et équitable des minorités ethniques, une conscience sociale plus manifeste et la mise en vigueur de programmes d'action positive figurait à l'ordre du jour de la plupart des gouvernements. Cette vague de libéralisme a eu des retombées importantes sur le sort des Amérindiens. La philosophie sous-jacente aux nouvelles politiques amérindiennes reposait sur la reconnaissance du fait que les Canadiens se doivent de réparer les erreurs de leurs ancêtres et de trouver des moyens d'augmenter la participation du peuple amérindien à la société canadienne. Les gouvernements ont lancé nombre de programmes d'emploi et de formation et progressivement ont commencé à influencer le secteur privé, voir même à l'obliger, à faire de même.

Au début des années soixante-dix, le chômage n'avait pas atteint les proportions incontrôlables que nous connaissons aujourd'hui et par conséquent la résistance à cette pression fut beaucoup plus faible qu'elle ne l'aurait été dans une période de contrainte économique. D'ailleurs les chefs d'entreprises se sensibilisaient au climat social de l'époque et étaient très conscients du rôle qu'ils avaient à jouer afin de démontrer que leurs responsabilités allaient au-delà de mettre au point des stratégies visant à augmenter les bénéfices. Les directeurs de personnel devenaient directeurs de ressources humaines et à mesure que le Canada s'avançait dans les années quatre-vingts, les départements de relations publiques se transformaient en départements d'affaires publiques. Les travailleurs ou les employés commençaient à être considérés comme ressources humaines. C'est devant cette toile de fond que des programmes d'emploi destinés aux Amérindiens ont vu le jour.

Cette étude examine un échantillon de programmes d'emploi mis en vigueur dans le secteur privé au cours de la dernière décennie dont l'objet est d'augmenter la participation du peuple amérindien au marché de travail canadien. Nos recherches se limitent aux villes de l'ouest canadien pour deux raisons : les populations amérindiennes y sont prépondérantes et nous avons pu y repérer un nombre important d'entreprises qui ont lancé des programmes d'emploi à l'intention des Amérindiens. Aussi, nous étions convaincus que les résultats de nos recherches dans les dix entreprises qui ont servi d'études de cas seraient généralisables à travers le Canada. Les études de cas ont été choisies selon notre certitude qu'elles reflétaient l'éventail de programmes en vigueur dans toutes sortes d'entreprises.

Au chapitre premier on définit le terme " Amérindien urbain " et on présente les objectifs de l'étude. L'objet principal de cette recherche est d'augmenter la visibilité des programmes d'emploi actuels qui réussissent à intéresser les Amérindiens et à les garder parmi la population active. La raison d'être de l'étude, la méthodologie utilisée et les caractéristiques générales des dix entreprises faisant l'objet d'études de cas y sont également présentées. Deux autres objectifs de l'étude consistent à souligner les nouvelles tendances émergeant de la participation des Amérindiens à la population active et à servir d'exemple aux entreprises qui ont en main tous les attributs nécessaires à la création de programmes semblables mais qui n'ont pas encore agi en ce sens. Les six chapitres suivants ne portent que sur les résultats de recherche dans six des dix entreprises consultées car les renseignements obtenus dans quatre entreprises ne justifiaient pas des chapitres distincts. Il faut quand même souligner que les programmes dans ces quatre entreprises n'étaient qu'à l'étape de la conceptualisation.

Headstart Employment Corporation est un organisme à but non-lucratif mis sur pied par la Saskatchewan Power Corporation; il offre la formation pré-apprentissage, la formation académique et éventuellement un emploi permanent à des candidats qui ne possèdent pas certains antécédents académiques, qu'ils soient d'origine amérindienne ou qu'ils soient désavantagés. Une moitié des candidats de Headstart est d'origine amérindienne et l'autre ne l'est pas. Ce programme a été lancé en 1978 et n'a cessé de croître depuis lors. Son expansion est due à plusieurs facteurs : les dirigeants de la Saskatchewan Power Corporation l'appuie fortement et mettent leurs ressources financières et humaines à sa disposition; le coordonnateur de Headstart a déjà travaillé avec les Amérindiens de la Saskatchewan et il exerce la profession de travailleur social; le recrutement se déroule partout en Saskatchewan et les stagiaires ont une opportunité de travailler près de leur domicile; les dirigeants d'une école de formation professionnelle font partie du Conseil d'administration de Headstart; et le ratio de surveillants à stagiaires est de un à deux. Il est important de souligner cependant que puisque l'on mise sérieusement sur la réussite de Headstart, les postulants indésirables sont éliminés dès le processus de sélection. Headstart est à la recherche de candidats qui peuvent démontrer qu'ils se sont déjà adaptés à la société dominante.

Native Metal Industries (NMI) a été fondée en 1970 suite à l'initiative du président de Interprovincial Steel and Pipe Corporation (IPSCO) qui était convaincu que les Amérindiens pouvaient, avec des matériaux fournis par IPSCO, diriger leur propre entreprise de récupération de la ferraille. Les gouvernements du Canada et de la Saskatchewan ont contribué les sommes nécessaires à lancer l'entreprise et la Saskatchewan Economic Development Corporation a cédé un terrain à l'usage de la nouvelle entreprise. Native Metal Industries peut être définie comme un atelier protégé où les Amérindiens qui n'ont jamais travaillé dans un milieu industriel peuvent être formés en tant que soudeurs. De 1970 à 1975, l'entreprise était gérée entièrement par les Amérindiens mais des querelles intestines entre les membres des deux associations amérindiennes constituant sa main-d'oeuvre, l'ont amenée presque à la faillite. En 1976, on engagea un administrateur non-amérindien dont le mandat était de mettre au point de nouvelles mesures administratives et d'éliminer une accumulation de mauvaises dettes; les gouvernements ont versé des fonds supplémentaires, les employés se sont syndiqués et un conseil d'administration fut élu.

Théoriquement, NMI est la propriété des Amérindiens puisque ses actionnaires sont tous des employés amérindiens, mais en réalité l'entreprise est administrée par un conseil d'administration dont quatre membres ne sont pas Amérindiens. Les administrateurs prennent toutes les décisions financières et les profits lorsqu'il y en a, doivent être réinvestis dans l'entreprise. L'hypothèse sur laquelle NMI a été basée veut que les Amérindiens soient mieux placés pour diriger une entreprise amérindienne. Les faits ont démontré cependant que la bonne volonté ne peut pas remplacer le manque d'expérience administrative.

Syncrude Canada Limited embauche des Amérindiens depuis son incorporation en 1972, mais ce n'est qu'en 1978 que son département de " Native Development " a été officiellement mis sur pied. Le premier mandat de ce département a été de formuler un plan quinquennal précisant les services et les programmes dont pourraient bénéficier les employés amérindiens, ainsi que les entrepreneurs amérindiens oeuvrant dans les régions environnant les installations de Syncrude.

Les membres du personnel du départment de " Native Development " (qui sont presque tous Amérindiens) ont mis en vigueur des programmes et des services au fur et à mesure que les besoins des employés amérindiens se faisaient sentir. Plusieurs programmes ont été créés dans le but de combler les lacunes académiques de certains membres de la communauté ou de l'entreprise. Cet objectif est dû à la conviction des dirigeants de Syncrude à l'effet que l'éducation facilite l'égalité et que c'est au niveau de la communauté que cette idée doit s'implanter. Par conséquent, Syncrude tente à travers une variété de programmes de toucher les jeunes et de leur transmettre la valeur de l'éducation. Les programmes de Syncrude soulignent également l'importance de la nécessité d'un changement d'attitudes de la part des Amérindiens et des non-Amérindiens afin qu'ils puissent travailler ensemble harmonieusement. Les colloques d'appréciation culturelle ont été créés dans le but de promouvoir cet objectif.

Plusieurs facteurs expliquent le succès des programmes amérindiens de Syncrude et en voici les plus importants : l'engagement de son premier président vis-à-vis le peuple amérindien; l'incitation de la direction à l'effet qu'un employé amérindien cadre entreprenne une analyse de programmes amérindiens mis en vigueur ailleurs au Canada et aux États-Unis. (Le 'plan d'action' fut le résultat de ce travail; on y recommande la création de programmes d'adaptation urbaine, de consultation familiale et de formation sociale et culturelle.) La signature en 1976 du " Indian Opportunities Agreement " (convention d'opportunités pour les Amérindiens) par " The Indian Association of Alberta " (l'Association amérindienne de l'Alberta), le gouvernement du Canada et Syncrude; et finalement le fait que le département de " Native Development " est presque totalement géré par des employés amérindiens. À notre connaissance, Syncrude offre l'ensemble le plus complet de programmes et de services à l'intention des Amérindiens qui soit disponible au Canada.

Le président de NOVA, an Alberta Corporation, a été l'agent catalyseur de l'engagement de cette société vis-à-vis le recrutement du peuple amérindien; depuis 1973 il se consacre à augmenter la participation des Amérindiens à toutes les phases d'opération de l'entreprise. Au début, NOVA visait un quota d'employés amérindiens qui devait refléter leur pourcentage dans la population de l'Alberta. Lorsque cet objectif fut réalisé en 1980, on constata qu'il était en quelque sorte arbitraire de se limiter à des chiffres. À l'origine, l'entreprise percevait le peuple amérindien en tant que ressource locale dont elle avait la responsabilité morale d'embaucher; aujourd'hui on reconnaît que le peuple amérindien est une ressource importante qui doit être recherchée en raison de sa compétence. D'autres facteurs importants contribuent à expliquer le succès de NOVA : depuis le lancement du programme de recrutement amérindien en 1976, un agent de liaison amérindien fait partie du personnel et il est chargé d'entretenir des contacts avec les communautés amérindiennes et de venir en aide aux employés amérindiens; le " Opportunity Measures Plan " (Plan d'opportunités), dont l'objet était de guider la mise en vigueur de la partie albertaine du projet de construction du gazoduc de l'Alaska, a été élaboré par un Amérindien; l'Administration du pipeline du Nord précisait les conditions à respecter afin d'améliorer le statut socio-économique des Amérindiens de l'Alberta; l'Alberta Vocational Centre (Centre de formation professionnelle), situé à Grouard, offre des cours d'adaptation urbaine et de formation dans divers métiers; NOVA a intégré à sa main d'oeuvre les stagiaires amérindiens qui devaient participer à la construction du pipeline; NOVA reconnaît l'importance d'une formation particulière visant les directeurs et les surveillants dont relèveraient les stagiaires amérindiens.

Puisque NOVA veut éviter l'insuccès, ses mesures de recrutement sont très sélectives. On accorde la préférence aux candidats qui ont démontré une certaine stabilité d'emploi. Peu d'importance est attachée aux critères de la formation académique, mais les candidats qui démontrent le potentiel à savoir accomplir le travail sont les premiers choisis. NOVA tente également d'établir une correspondance entre les compétences des individus et les tâches à accomplir : les individus possédant le même genre de compétences sont placés dans le même genre de fonctions. Cette stratégie permet d'entrevoir une diminution des conflits entre les employés amérindiens et les autres. Le Manitoba Telephone System (MTS) a mis sur pied deux programmes qui ouvrent l'accès aux Amérindiens à des opportunités d'emploi. Le premier, " Equal Employment Opportunity " (EEO) (Égalité des chances d'emploi), est un programme d'action positive qui fonctionne depuis 1975; l'autre, " New

Careers " (Carrières nouvelles), est une initiative du ministère du Travail et de la main-d'oeuvre du Manitoba et a fonctionné au MTS pendant deux ans, soit en 1976 et en 1977. L'objet du programme d'Égalité des chances d'emploi est d'augmenter le nombre de femmes, de personnes handicapées et d'Amérindiens au sein du MTS afin de refléter plus adéquatement le pourcentage qu'ils occupent dans la population du Manitoba. Le EEO est un plan d'action quinquennal qui comporte les mesures suivantes : l'identification des obstacles à trouver un emploi et leur suppression; la création de programmes de formation spécialisée; la formation d'intervieweurs et de surveillants; l'évaluation des communications écrites de l'entreprise et leur reformulation en vue d'éliminer tout préjugé ou stéréotype; la diffusion à grande échelle de la politique MTS de l'égalité des chances d'emploi.

" New Careers " est un programme de formation au travail et de perfectionnement académique fondé sur deux hypothèses : les adultes ont le droit d'avoir accès à un emploi et la pauvreté ne résulte pas d'une faiblesse personnelle innée mais plutôt de contraintes économiques, sociales ou géographiques qui empêchent plusieurs individus de s'intégrer à la population active. L'objet d'un programme " New Careers " est de restructurer les définitions de tâches et de former les candidats selon les exigences précises de la tâche à accomplir sans pour cela diminuer la qualité du rendement. La direction de MTS appuyait sérieusement le programme " New Careers " et avait engagé un surveillant amérindien dès son lancement. Le programme a été discontinué temporairement à cause de coupures budgétaires au sein du gouvernement manitobain, mais des discussions se poursuivent sur la manière d'améliorer le programme lorsqu'il sera rétabli.

La division manitobaine de la société INCO Metals embauche des Amérindiens depuis 1960. Ce n'est cependant qu'en 1972 que INCO a créé un programme d'emploi nordique afin de recruter et de former la main-d'oeuvre disponible dans les communautés environnant Thompson. INCO a établi un programme essentiellement de recrutement sous la direction d'un coordonnateur amérindien, offrant au nouvel employé l'aide nécessaire à son installation urbaine. INCO n'a pas créé des programmes spéciaux à l'intention de ses employés amérindiens, mais dirige ceux qui ont besoin d'aide vers les agences pertinentes dans la ville de Thompson. Lors de campagnes de recrutement dans les communautés amérindiennes, le coordonnateur travaille en collaboration avec un agent amérindien du ministère du Travail et de la main-d'oeuvre dont la fonction principale est d'aider les candidats à faire la transition entre leur communauté d'origine et un centre urbain. Les candidats doivent subir une période de formation industrielle et les Amérindiens, une fois embauchés, sont traités de la même manière que les autres employés puisqu'ils sont présumés avoir la même expérience de travail. Après une année d'emploi, les employés ont accès à une période de formation au Keewatin Community College, qu'ils soient Amérindiens ou non.

Le dernier chapitre présente vingt-six points qui, selon l'opinion du chercheur, mérite que ceux qui s'intéressent à toute facette de programmes d'emploi à l'intention des Amérindiens s'y attardent. Les suggestions résultent d'une analyse du fonctionnement de chacune des dix entreprises en question. Quelques-unes démontrent des mesures déjà établies et d'autres tentent de combler des lacunes importantes à l'étape de l'élaboration de programmes. Ces idées représentent l'ensemble des facteurs significatifs et innovateurs que l'on retrouve à l'analyse de programmes " à succès ". Des progrès valables ont été fait dans ce domaine et on espère que la diffusion de cette information à un vaste auditoire contribuera à une meilleure planification de programmes.

1: Introduction

Parameters

This research project was undertaken to demonstrate the types of organizational arrangements that are conducive to the establishment and maintenance of a Native-employment program. To this end, this study describes and analyses programs in the corporate sector designed to facilitate the entry of people of Indian ancestry into the Canadian labour force. The need to undertake this project became evident during a series of meetings held in Canada's four Western provinces in 1978 in order to develop a research program in collaboration with Native people. These meetings were attended by representatives of Native organizations, municipal, provincial and federal government officials, and businessmen who had some professional experience in interacting with Native people residing in urban centres. The meetings confirmed that many companies, large and small, were in various stages of initiating or managing programs to accommodate Native people. The suggestion was made that an investigation of the application and success of these programs would prove worthwhile.

For the purposes of this study, the term 'urban Native' refers to all people of Indian ancestry living in urban centres. This includes registered Indians (Treaty and non-Treaty), non-registered, or non-status, Indians, and Métis. The current meaning of the term 'urban Native' has been captured in the following definition:

> The urban Indian is identified not by his reserve affiliation or by his treaty status or by his socio-economic position. He or she is identified by ethnicity and heritage and by the fact of having made a conscious choice to maintain and reinforce that ethnicity...while living in the city.[1]

Urbanization is a more recent phenomenon for Native people than for most Canadians. Indeed, it is only within the last fifteen years that Native people have migrated to cities in appreciable numbers. It is estimated that the Native residents of cities such as Winnipeg, Regina, Saskatoon, Calgary, Edmonton and Vancouver make up between 5 and 20 per cent of their total population. The migration and settlement of this group create some strain for traditional urban institutions, but more for Native people themselves and for their institutions. This study will investigate collaborative programs that some companies have developed to alleviate some of the strains in the area of employment, arising from Native urban settlement.

Objectives

The objectives of this study are, first, to present and document programs that exist in the corporate sector to accommodate people of Indian ancestry and, secondly, to examine the characteristics of these programs: their goals, the policies that underlie them or that have emerged from them, the conditions under which they were created, and the processes of their implementation. The study will describe and analyse various types of programs that have been implemented, some that are ongoing and some that have been discontinued. It will seek to determine the role of the companies in initiating and managing these programs and to suggest what can be learned from their experiences. Why, for instance, did certain companies decide to create a Native-employment program? Was it to demonstrate a sense of social responsibility, to respond to legislation, to create a skilled labour pool, or to take advantage of available human resources?

While answers to these questions may prove illuminating, this study was not launched only to increase awareness of existing programs to promote Native employment, but with the hope of meeting another set of objectives, as well:

- To inform Native people of the opportunities that are available to them
- To identify emerging trends in the employment of Native people
- To serve as a catalyst to firms that have not yet created Native-employment programs.

Such programs do exist in the corporate sector, yet they have very little visibility. By disproving some widely held myths and removing some popular stereotypes, such as "Companies don't want to hire Native people", or "Native people don't want to hold down steady jobs, anyway", we shall attempt to highlight the Native-employment issue.

Some of the programs examined in this study may be assimilative, and others may be integrative. These terms should be distinguished, since they are very often, mistakenly, used synonymously. In the Native-employment context, 'assimilation' refers to the deliberate attempt to formulate policies that force a minority group to assume the characteristics of the dominant group in order to gain general acceptance. 'Integration', on the other hand, refers to an attempt to facilitate or accommodate the inclusion of a minority group into a dominant group, while respecting the minority's culture and identity.   Native people strongly resist assimilative policies because these call for a radical abandonment of their traditions, life-style, identity and culture. Integrative policies promote change accomplished with minimal tension both in the dominant group and in the minority group when the two come into contact with each other.[2]

Rationale

Native people migrate to cities principally to find jobs.   Diminishing economic opportunities on many reserves force them to look to cities for better prospects.   However, many Native people are not prepared for an urban environment.   Migration and integration into a new culture are difficult processes of adjustment; when a person's physical characteristics differ from those typical of members of the dominant culture, he or she inevitably becomes more vulnerable to prejudice and discrimination, and the processes take on larger proportions.   There are, of course, many other barriers that a Native person must cope with in the urban context, but discrimination is perhaps the most overwhelming.

Once in the city, many Native people learn that their education is insufficient to assure them   employment, that their training does not match the available jobs, that they are not part of a job-finding network,[3] that the various levels of government are embroiled in jurisdictional disputes to determine which is responsible for them, that housing is expensive and difficult to find.   Consequently, the proportion of unemployed Native people is much higher than the corresponding figure for the general population, a situation that increases the level of social tensions in an urban environment. Unemployment in the city, where one is faced with the problem of coping with a 'foreign' and often hostile environment, can be much harsher than unemployment on the reserve, where a person can rely, to some extent, at least, on family support. Yet for many, the reserve offers little or no hope of attaining an acceptable standard of living. Natives are often caught up in the bitter choice of facing poverty in their own communities or poverty in the city.

Approach

The case-study approach was judged the best way to illustrate the range of programs available to Native people in Western Canada. A brief questionnaire was sent to more than 300 companies, located in Manitoba, Saskatchewan, Alberta and British Columbia, that met the following criteria: they employed at least 100 people, and they were located in an urban centre. Provincial corporations were included in this preliminary survey because they were major employers, and some of them had implemented Affirmative Action programs that included Native people. A letter, addressed to the president of each firm, accompanied the questionnaire and explained the purpose of the project. The questionnaire was designed to answer three questions:

- Did these firms have in place programs to promote the integration of people of Indian ancestry into their work force?
- What was the nature of these programs?
- Would these firms be willing to participate in this study?

Of the 100 companies that responded, twenty-five had Native people on their staffs and were willing to collaborate in this project. The remaining seventy-five expressed a strong interest in the results of the study, but were not in a position to participate either because they had no Native people on staff, or because they had not yet developed programs to accommodate them. Two companies, Revelstoke Companies Ltd. and Asamera Oil Corporation Ltd., made an unsolicited financial contribution to the project.

Ten companies were selected from the possible twenty-five, according to the following criteria:

- They represented various regions of the West.
- They covered as many industrial sectors as possible.
- They varied in the nature of programs offered, type of ownership, and company size.

Ten was considered a manageable number in view of the budget and time limitations of the study. Two firms were selected in each of Manitoba, Saskatchewan and Alberta, where programs were sufficiently developed to permit substantial observations. This was not the situation in British Columbia, where programs were in preliminary stages of development. Four companies were selected there, one of which preferred to remain anonymous, but upon investigation it was decided that the findings were not sufficient to merit a separate chapter.

Nine firms that agreed to participate in this study are:

- The Saskatchewan Power Corporation
- Native Metal Industries
- Syncrude Canada Limited
- NOVA, an Alberta Corporation
- The Manitoba Telephone System
- INCO Metals Company (Manitoba Division)
- Canadian Cellulose Company Ltd.
- Westcoast Transmission Company Ltd.
- Weyerhaeuser Canada Ltd.

Two of these companies are provincial Crown corporations, six are publicly owned, one is of mixed ownership,[4] and one is owned by its employees, who are of Indian ancestry. One of the publicly owned companies is a subsidiary of an American corporation; one is a subsidiary of a Canadian corporation; one is part of a multinational corporate network; and the other three are Canadian-owned corporations.

Some of the Native programs represent joint efforts on the part of the federal government and a company or corporation; others represent joint efforts between a company and a provincial government; some are tripartite in nature, in that the federal government, a provincial government and a company are their sponsors; and others are strictly the result of one particular company's endeavours. The numbers of employees in all these companies range between seventy[5] and 5000. Some companies have been running a successful program since 1976; others were then running programs that have now been discontinued; others were just getting programs into operation; and still others were in the early stages of program design. Some companies are located in small urban centres, and others are located in large cities.

The industrial sectors that some of these ten companies represent are resource based or resource oriented: mining, oil-and-gas production, forest products, transportation of oil and gas, pipeline construction. Other companies are service oriented: they provide telephone services and electricity. Some of the companies manufacture heavy equipment and process materials.

The programs operating in these companies focus primarily on recruitment and on-the-job training, but also include instruction in life-skills, relocation, academic upgrading, pre-employment training, career development, and cultural awareness. Table 1 (p. 8, below) illustrates the diversity of cases under study.

Framework

A research design was developed to provide the project with a framework to facilitate the interview process and the analysis of information. The unit of analysis chosen was a 'program package' designed to accommodate Native people in the corporate sector. The study focuses on the characteristics of programs rather than on the individuals concerned and

Table 1: Characteristics of Companies Selected to Illustrate Variety of Native Programs in the Canadian Corporate Sector

Province	Company	Location	Size [a]	Ownership	Programs	Sponsors	Activity
Manitoba	• INCO Metals Company	Thompson	2 500	Public	• Recruitment • Relocation	INCO Metals, Manitoba Government	Mining
	• Manitoba Telephone System	Winnipeg	4 665	Crown Corporation	• Academic upgrading • On-the-job training	Manitoba Government	Telephone service
Saskatchewan	• Saskatchewan Power Corporation	Regina	3 200	Crown Corporation	• Academic upgrading • On-the-job training	SPC,[b] Saskatchewan Government and Federal Government	Electricity
	• Native Metals Industries	Regina	70	Employee-owned	• On-the-job training	Federal Govt., Saskatchewan Government, IPSCO[c]	Metal transformation
Alberta	• NOVA, an Alberta Corporation	Calgary	1 264	Public	• Recruitment • Life skills	NOVA	Transmission of gas
	• Syncrude Canada Ltd.	Fort McMurray	3 300	Mixed[d]	• Recruitment • Life-Skills • On-the-job training • Cultural awareness	Syncrude	Crude oil extraction
British Columbia[e]	• Canadian Cellulose Company Ltd.	Vancouver	2 500	Public	• Recruitment • Training	Canadian Cellulose	Forest products
	• Westcoast Transmission Co. Ltd.	Vancouver	727	Public	• Recruitment	Westcoast Transmission	Pipeline transportation of natural gas
	• Weyerhaeuser Canada Ltd.	Kamloops	2 000	Public	• At conceptual stage	Weyerhaeuser	Kraft pulp Lumber
	• Company "X"	Vancouver	1 700	Public	• Recruitment • Training	Company "X"	Manufacturing and sales

Notes

a. Number of employees.

b. Saskatchewan Power Corporation.

c. Interprovincial Steel and Pipe Corporation.

d. Federal and Provincial governments and private elements share the ownership of Syncrude Canada Ltd.

e. The information obtained about the four companies located in British Columbia was insufficient to warrant a separate chapter, as had been originally planned.

is therefore largely descriptive. Though the history, objectives, implementation and functioning of each program are given considerable attention, an attempt was also made to elicit information about indicators of participants' successful adaptation, such as job stability, productivity, interpersonal relations and job satisfaction. It was difficult to obtain comparable data in these areas because these measures are, for the most part, subjective, and relevant company records have not been kept in any consistent fashion. Nevertheless, data were obtained that reveal pertinent features of the success or failure of specific programs.

Methodology

It seemed probable that the best source of data to meet the objectives of this study would be extensive interviews with as many individuals as possible who have been or are involved in a given aspect of a Native-employment program. In response to a personal letter to a company president, the researcher was usually referred to the person or persons responsible for the company's Native programs. The researcher then contacted these individuals by telephone, to explain the objectives and scope of the study and to determine the numbers of interviews to be carried out and the conditions under which they would take place. An interview schedule consisting of some 200 questions based on the research design was developed to guide the discussions.

On this basis, sixty persons were interviewed, twenty of whom were of Indian ancestry. The largest number of individuals interviewed in a particular company was eleven; the lowest was one. The longest time spent with any one company was two and a half days; the average time was one and a half days. Interviews lasted from thirty minutes to three hours each and were tape-recorded. In a few interviews, it was possible to cover the entire questionnaire, but generally only those questions applicable to an individual's particular role were asked. Only one person refused to allow his comments to be recorded on tape; two other interviews were not tape-recorded because they took place in public places where the noise level was too high.

A Caution

A decision was made early in this project about the identification of case-studies. Anonymity might have permitted a more critical evaluation of the programs, but this approach was rejected in order to achieve one of the most important objectives of this study, that is, visibility of Native-employment programs. Readers must know where the reported experiences were taking place. Anonymity of respondents was, however, respected, and no statement in this report is to be attributed to a particular individual.

It seemed advantageous to try to ensure the co-operation of both companies and Native employees in order to collect as much information as possible about the design and operation of programs rather than to risk that co-operation and thus reduce the degree of information that would be forthcoming. Thus the researcher was not at liberty to choose her respondents. Since they were selected by management, however, there was a danger that she would hear only the 'company line'. (It is unrealistic to think that an employee is going to 'open up' on company policy and practices in the presence of an outsider equipped with a tape-recorder.) For this reason, the researcher tried to interview as many individuals as possible who had a role to play in the implementation or functioning of the same program.

The information contained in this report was current as of 30 June 1980; changes in company policy, procedure and personnel after that date are not reflected.

Notes

1.   Larry Krotz, *Urban Indians, The Strangers in Canada's Cities* (Edmonton, Hurtig Publishers Ltd., 1980).

2.   Ken Svenson, "Indian and Métis Issues in Saskatchewan to 2001" (December 1978).

3.   Brian Hill, "A Proposed Strategy to Enhance the Access of Indian People to Existing Jobs" (Regina, 1978).

4.   See Table 1, note d.

5.   At one time this company employed over 100 people, which made it eligible for inclusion in this study.

2: The Saskatchewan Power Corporation

Characteristics and Setting

The Saskatchewan Power Corporation (SPC) is a Crown corporation created in 1949 to produce, transmit, and distribute electricity and natural gas throughout the Province of Saskatchewan. SPC has 3000 employees, 600 of whom occupy management positions; 1200 belong to the International Brotherhood of Electrical Workers, and 1200 belong to the Atomic Workers International Union. There are approximately 150 persons of Indian ancestry working for SPC, but none occupies a management position. This figure is merely an estimate, since employee records do not indicate ethnic or racial origin.

SPC began hiring Native people in the mid-1960s, but it was not until 1977 that the numbers of Native employees grew appreciably because of the creation of the Headstart Employment Corporation (HEC). In hiring its first Native employees, SPC initiated an 'affirmative action' program well before it became law in 1979, under the new Saskatchewan Human Rights Code. In this chapter we shall examine the Headstart Employment Corporation.

The Headstart Employment Corporation

History

Early in 1977, Canada's Manpower and Immigration Job Creation Branch drafted a proposal to create employment opportunities for Natives living in Regina.   This project was to involve the City of Regina, the University of Regina, the Saskatchewan Power Corporation, and other companies; LEAP[1] funds were to be requested. A Native organization opposed this proposal because the target group was to be urban Natives, and the organization's leaders wanted the project to focus strictly on Treaty Indians.

At the same time, SPC management elaborated a proposal that focused on job training and academic upgrading for Native people, rather than on the disadvantaged who, they considered, were being serviced adequately by other agencies. SPC's objective was to hire a pool of fifty Native workers, who would be part of the work-force for eight months of the year, and who would attend educational institutions for the remaining four months. On successful completion of this program, trainees would be offered permanent jobs within SPC. It was considered that this program would be more effective if it were run by a Native person. SPC, the federal government, and the Saskatchewan government were to fund the program, each contributing a third of its support. The intention was that all contracts signed by SPC should stipulate that a certain percentage of employees be of Indian ancestry, and that Native organizations play a major role in promoting the program. These plans never materialized, but they opened the doors to further discussions, in 1977, between SPC officials and representatives of Canada Employment and Immigration, then called 'Canada Manpower'.

SPC and Canada Manpower agreed, in 1977, to set the wheels in motion for the creation of a non-profit organization. Its aim would be to offer   pre-apprenticeship   training   and   academic   upgrading   to disadvantaged individuals, both those of Indian ancestry and others. This organization was expected to become self-financing by contracting its services to SPC and, eventually, to other companies requiring linemen and workers with related skills, on a fee-for-service basis; its revenues were to be reinvested in expansion and training. Start-up funds were provided by SPC, the Community Employment Strategy Program,[2] and the Canada Manpower Industrial Training Program (CMITP). This program was launched 28 March 1978 as 'Headstart Employment Corporation'.

The Headstart Board of Directors consisted of the Director of Adult Basic Education at Regina Plains Community College, a retired SPC employee of Indian ancestry, who had business experience, and the manager of SPC's Management Development and Training Division. A Canada Employment Special Program consultant was named as co-ordinator and consultant to the Board. In April 1978 the Headstart Employment Corporation was incorporated under the Business Corporations Act, and in June 1978 a formal contract was signed between the Saskatchewan Power Corporation and the Headstart Employment Corporation to clarify their financial arrangements.

According to Headstart's articles of incorporation, the number of directors could have ranged between two and five, but at a meeting of the Headstart Board on 9 October 1979, it was set at five. Two new members were elected to the Board in 1979: a Chief of a Saskatchewan reserve, who was also an administrator of the Federation of Saskatchewan Indians, and a private consultant, who was Chairman of the Interdepartmental Committee Secretariat of the Department of Indian Affairs in Regina. One member of the Board resigned in 1979 when he accepted the job of co-ordinator/consultant for Headstart.

Objectives

When the Headstart Employment Corporation (HEC) was launched, SPC had long been giving attention to the problems of the underprivileged segment of the labour market and had been re-evaluating and readjusting its policies accordingly. Headstart, which is, in essence, a program to equalize opportunities, was the result of an eight-year process during which a company's philosophy with respect to Native people gradually evolved. Headstart's first mandate was to:

> ...promote the training and satisfactory employment of urban natives; establish a "Headstart crew...."
>
> ...train participants to a basic skill level that will allow them to proceed in the regular SPC induction crews....
>
> ...be responsible for identifying individual barriers and developing plans to eliminate these barriers, as well as providing continuous support to these individuals during the work-situation phase; develop training and evaluation mechanisms in conjunction with the target group, employers, federal/provincial governments and other interested community representatives....[3]

Originally Headstart's primary objective was to provide academic upgrading and skills training to urban Natives. A second objective was to contract out the services of its trainees to other firms: in this way, individuals would not necessarily be limited to working for one company, and the outside contracts made by the group would contribute to Headstart's economic independence. In addition the Headstart planners hoped that this program would stimulate other firms to take similar initiatives.

At the end of 1979, Headstart's Board of Directors realigned its objectives as follows:

● That Headstart include 50 per cent Native people and 50 per cent disadvantaged people

- That more stringent methods of selecting candidates be applied, based on an individual's motivation, aptitude and ability
- That Headstart function all year round
- That a comprehensive training program be formalized
- That students be referred to colleges in all areas of Saskatchewan for their academic upgrading
- That more companies in Saskatchewan be induced to award contracts to the Headstart Employment Corporation.

Implementation and Functioning

At a meeting on 25 January 1978 between SPC and Canada Manpower representatives, the possibility of organizing a crew to work and train within SPC's Electrical Distribution Division was discussed and agreed to. This crew would consist of five or six persons in disadvantaged situations, who had displayed the potential to become linemen. They would receive pre-apprenticeship training on the job and academic upgrading in vocational schools in Saskatchewan; if successful, they would move on to join an induction crew as apprentice linemen; their goal was to become journeymen in the line trade.

A former SPC lineman, with several years' experience in the line trade and in social services, was hired on a contract basis as the Headstart organizer/supervisor; he was not of Indian ancestry. With the assistance of a Canada Employment representative, he screened and selected candidates and, when the work crews were constituted, gave them direction, training and counselling.

Criteria of eligibility for Headstart

In order to be admitted to Headstart, a candidate must be a Native or a non-Native who has had to cope with some form of social handicap, have an educational disqualification, and be employable. The term 'educational disqualification', which was coined by a Headstart co-ordinator, means that the candidate must lack certain educational qualifications: for example, he may not have reached Grade-12 level in algebra, physics or trigonometry. Candidates may be chosen who have achieved only a Grade-10 standing in these subjects, but, for those who have not gone beyond this scholastic level, academic upgrading takes longer.

Methods of recruitment

Headstart candidates either apply directly to SPC's Personnel Department, where they are referred to the Headstart co-ordinator, or they are referred to him by Canada Employment Centres or by one of the provincial community colleges. The co-ordinator provides information to Native groups and to band councils and Native leaders on an informal basis, but the information usually reaches the reserves by word of mouth. In 1979 the Headstart co-ordinator interviewed 125 applicants; in 1980, this figure rose to 200.

Union involvement

The International Brotherhood of Electrical Workers (IBEW) was tolerant of the Headstart activities in the first two years of its operation. However, pressure was exerted on the union by its members because they did not understand why individuals who were doing the same work as they were, at the same wage rates, in addition to being paid while attending courses, were not required to pay union dues. Subsequently, the union, which had been invited to join the Headstart Board, and which had been keeping a low profile in this venture, began to show some concern and to suggest that Headstart employees be unionized.

Negotiations for the unionization of Headstart employees began in 1980 and were relatively smooth, perhaps because there is a shared goal between the IBEW and the Headstart Employment Corporation: they both exist to improve the workers' conditions. The IBEW obtained a certification order for HEC employees in early 1981.

Work crews

First year (1978/1979). The first Headstart crew was selected by Canada Employment in the winter of 1978 and began training on March 28 of that year. It consisted of five Natives and two non-Natives, under the direction of an organizer/supervisor. Following a brief period of preliminary training, the crew began productive work in power-line-related activities: salvaging, right-of-way clearance, construction and repair of power-line structures, and so on. Between 1 May and 8 December 1978, it generated revenues totalling $101 555. These revenues were 35 per cent higher than the amounts that had been targeted.

Of the original 1978 crew of seven, only four members remained with Headstart throughout the year and enrolled, in January 1979, in Regina Plains Community College to complete Grade 12. Two of the other three original members were terminated in the summer of 1978 because of personal problems, and the third was hired by SPC as an equipment operator; he resigned because he was unwilling to relocate. In the summer of 1978, an attempt was made to replace the three crew members who had left Headstart, but it was unsuccessful; two of the replacements were terminated because of personal problems affecting job performance, and the other resigned, after having worked for a time as an equipment operator at SPC; again, this last crew member resigned because he was unwilling to relocate.

Second year (1979/1980). Though the 1978 experience involved few trainees, the Headstart Board considered it a moderate success, since four individuals remained with the program until they had completed their academic upgrading; three of them went on to join the SPC induction crew in the summer of 1979, and one joined one of the 1979

Headstart crews. Moreover the revenues that Headstart generated were higher than expected. The Board, therefore, decided to expand the program to two crews for 1979, with the provisos that screening and selection of candidates take into consideration their motivation and abilities, and that a more comprehensive training program be developed.

The structure of the Headstart crews in 1979/1980 was different from that of the previous year. In addition to hiring an experienced lineman to train and supervise crew members, Headstart took on two equipment operators with experience in crew supervision and training. The 1978/1979 experience showed that one supervisor was not sufficient to handle training and supervision of seven trainees, as well as the maintenance of vehicles and equipment. The first crew, located in Regina, consisted of a foreman, an equipment operator, a trainee in equipment operation, and eight trainee line workers, one of whom had been part of the 1978/1979 Headstart operation. The second crew, located in Prince Albert, included only seven trainee line workers. The sixteen new trainees were recruited from community colleges in Saskatchewan, from Canada Employment Centres, and through direct contact with the Headstart co-ordinator.

At the end of the work season, trainees were given a two-week paid vacation, from 14 December 1979 to 2 January 1980. Fourteen trainees entered various community colleges in January 1980 for academic upgrading: they received 75 per cent of their salary while attending classes from 2 January to 30 April 1980. Nine trainees graduated in the spring of 1980 and were taken into SPC's regular induction crew; four trainees returned to the Headstart crew for another season, since they had not completed all the course requirements for transfer into an induction crew; one was terminated because of personal problems.

Third year (1980/1981). After careful assessment of the 1979/1980 experience, the Headstart Board decided that it could manage four crews. In the early spring of 1980, the co-ordinator interviewed 200 candidates in all parts of Saskatchewan and selected thirty to attend a "Trade Explorations and Assessment Program". He had designed this program in collaboration with members of the Adult Basic Education Division of the Regina Plains Community College, where the training is carried out. This program is funded by Canada Employment, and its purpose is "to provide basic information and understanding to trainees as to the necessary technical, job, and life-skills components required to fulfill employment expectations as they related to the power line trade."[4] The program not only focuses on the line trade, but also provides the trainee with an opportunity to communicate with others and to familiarize himself with various pieces of equipment. The trainee is exposed to a variety of skills that he may be called upon to use in other trades, and he also learns what trades match his particular skills and interests.

Of the twenty-seven trainees in the 1980/1981 group (three of whom were carried over from the 1979/1980 operation), seventeen were of Indian ancestry. Nineteen members of the group entered community colleges in January 1981; three resigned for personal reasons, and five chose to work at the Regina power plant. Training in that plant relates to the utility trade, rather than to the line trade. The plant is basically a salvage- or destruction-of-plant-hardware operation, and workers do not have to be mobile, since both these activities occur at the same site. Moreover the work is less dangerous than the work of the line trade, since it does not involve high voltages, and the plant can accommodate larger crews because less supervision and fewer technical skills are required.

Indicators of Adaptation

Employee turnover

SPC has had Native employees since the early 1960s, but no data were available pertaining to the period preceding the creation of the Headstart Program in 1978. After HEC's first year of operation in 1978/1979, four of the original crew entered the SPC regular induction crew, after completing Grade 12 in the spring of 1979. After the second year (1979/1980), nine of the fourteen trainees completed Grade 12 and moved on to SPC induction crews; four trainees returned to the Headstart crew for another season, and one was terminated for personal reasons. After the third year (1980/1981), nineteen of the original crew of twenty-seven pursued an academic upgrading program; three resigned for personal reasons, and five continued to work as trainees in the Regina power plant.

Absenteeism

Absenteeism was a serious problem in the first year of the Headstart operation: of the six trainees who did not complete the program, four were terminated because of frequent absences related to alcoholism. These persons had been offered assistance by HEC staff and by members of their work crews and had had access to rehabilitation centres. As one manager pointed out, "An alcoholic can work, but when his state of drunkenness lasts twenty-four hours a day, it is impossible for him to be part of a work crew that depends on his presence to get the job done."

In the second year of the Headstart program, however, absenteeism was not as prevalent as in the first year.

Productivity

Headstart's financial statements for 1978 show that the first seven-man crew brought in revenues for work completed in the amount of $101 555. In 1979, two seven-man crews produced total revenues of $215 803. In 1980 it was expected that the four crews would bring in revenues of $500 000. Table 2, below, demonstrates the total productivity per crew on a yearly basis and the productivity per man if one divides total revenues by the number of members in each crew.

Table 2 shows that the productivity of Headstart crews has increased steadily, though not dramatically, over the life span of the program, in spite of the fact that the 1980 figure was projected.

Table 2: Productivity of Headstart Crews for the Years 1978, 1979, 1980

	Revenues	Number of Trainees	Revenue/Trainee
1978	$ 101 555	7 (1 crew)	$ 14 507
1979	$ 215 800	14 (2 crews)	$ 15 415
1980	$ 500 000	24 (4 crews)	$ 18 517

Participation

Headstart trainees interact on a daily basis with their foreman on work-related matters. They meet with the Headstart co-ordinator every two weeks. The only formal meeting that they attend is a monthly safety seminar. There seems to be no difference in the frequency of interaction, whether or not the supervisor or co-ordinator is a Native person. Since most trainees require extra support services, the co-ordinator assumes the role of social worker; he is often called upon to mediate between supervisors and trainees. He has found that Native trainees are more withdrawn and tend to listen during meetings, rather than to participate verbally. He has to make a point of gaining their confidence before he can be of any assistance to them on a personal basis.

Headstart is unique in that its employees must relate to one another in formal, as well as in social, settings. Because of the nature of their work, Headstart crews must work, travel, study and live together. As a result of these many opportunities for interaction, trainees come to know one another very well in a short period of time. Socializing is limited to members of individual crews because most of the work is done in remote areas; thus workers are generally isolated from other crews and from their families. Two trainees, one Native and one non-Native, reported that they had been invited into each other's homes during their vacation period, and both considered that they had been treated as members of the family. The Headstart trainees stated that when they were attending school for upgrading courses, teachers and other students recognized them as a unit and, though they did not feel out of place, they thought that they were being given preferential treatment. One supervisor was of the opinion that their 'special status' allowed them to experience a much-needed sense of freedom, but, more significantly, the respect they commanded motivated them to do well in their examinations.

Respondents' Observations

Though the eleven respondents believed that the Headstart program was meeting its major objective of providing employment and training to Native people and disadvantaged persons, they nevertheless made the following comments on its effectiveness:

- Though there are presently two persons of Indian ancestry on the Headstart Board, only one of them was involved from the beginning. There was no attempt at the conceptual stage or at the implementation stage, to involve Native organizations, band councils, or other Native representatives. While the Headstart program is acknowledged to be effective, it does reflect the biases of a non-Native male majority.
- The philosophy underlying the Headstart program is that Native

employees should be treated with the same respect as non-Native employees. Three trainees remarked that they considered they had special status when they were in vocational school, since they were allowed to make their own rules. They did not know whether they were respected, feared, or tolerated by teachers and other students, but they were certainly aware that they had not integrated into the student body. One can assume that the main effect of the Headstart program, in this instance, was to set the cohort of trainees apart from the other students. In any event, it would be interesting to learn whether this situation arose as a result of certain characteristics of the Headstart program, of the peculiarities of the academic setting, or of the collective behaviour of the Headstart trainees.

- Several respondents expressed concern that the Headstart program did not include women. As one of them pointed out, only when Headstart offers employment to women will it really be an equality-of-opportunity program.

- So far Headstart has not been a catalyst for the creation of similar programs in other companies, perhaps because its promoters are not over-confident of its success and have kept a low profile.

- Many of the initial difficulties in launching Headstart related to the problem of convincing middle management and other non-Native staff members that this program was not 'just another welfare activity'.

- The scope of Headstart is narrow, since it focuses on jobs in the trades. Most respondents believed that it should encompass management-training opportunities.

Conclusions

Though Headstart is a relatively recent program, it is growing steadily. We shall consider some of the features that may explain its success.

Management Support

The Saskatchewan Power Corporation's senior management and the Headstart Board of Directors have demonstrated a strong commitment to the Headstart concept. Furthermore, SPC's infrastructure permits the allocation of manpower and resources to the Headstart Employment Corporation whenever the need arises.

Native Experience

The Headstart Employment Corporation hired two co-ordinators who previously had worked with Native people, and who had a background in social work. In addition, two members of the HEC Board of Directors were of Indian ancestry. These factors may well have contributed to the trainees' development of a positive self-image and that, in turn, to their perseverance and success.

Selectivity Factor

The criteria of eligibility for Headstart are such that undesirable applicants are weeded out during the screening process: recruiters emphasize motivation, ability, and interest in the trades. If candidates display weaknesses in these areas, they are rejected. There seems to be a strong desire for Headstart to be successful and, consequently, an attempt is made to minimize risks by applying strict screening methods to candidate selection. Headstart accepts only those candidates who display at the outset those characteristics which indicate that they have already adapted to the dominant society. In other words, Headstart is successful largely because it eliminates the applicants who may have a particular problem in making this adaptation.

Ratio of Staff to Trainees

The ratio of staff to trainees is one to two; this figure is considered high. Training is provided almost on an individual basis and is thus completed more quickly than would be possible if a supervisor were responsible for several trainees.

Vocational Schools
Vocational schools in Saskatchewan participated actively in various ways: they chose representatives to sit on HEC's Board of Directors, provided academic upgrading to Headstart trainees, designed a Trades Exploration Course, and referred some of their students to the Headstart co-ordinator.

Proximity to Home Communities
The Headstart program attracts applicants because recruitment takes place all over Saskatchewan, and work crews may be located anywhere in the province. Candidates thus have a good chance of working close to their homes. Most trainees reported this to be an advantage.

Notes

1. Local Employment Assistance Programs (LEAP) were federally funded programs undertaken as a result of local initiatives.

2. A federal/provincial arrangement to "improve the delivery of employment-related services to persons experiencing particular and continuing difficulty in finding and keeping work."

3. Agreement between the Government of Canada (Employment and Immigration) and the Headstart Employment Corporation, Schedule "A", 1 April 1978.

4. D.J. Ash, "Trade Explorations and Assessment Program" (Regina, 21 March 1980).

3: Native Metal Industries Limited

Characteristics and Setting

Native Metal Industries (NMI) is located in Armour Siding, five kilometres from Regina. The company was created in 1970 because the Interprovincial Steel and Pipe Corporation (IPSCO), the Government of Saskatchewan, and the federal Department of Regional and Economic Expansion wished to set up a company whose main objective would be to offer to Native people employment and training in the scrap-iron-salvaging business. Since there is a link between IPSCO and NMI, we offer a few background notes on the former before we undertake a description of the latter.

IPSCO was incorporated in 1956 and constructed a steel mill in 1958. It is the largest steel company in Western Canada and produces 444 650 tonnes of steel per year. It is owned by the Province of Saskatchewan, Steel Alberta Limited, and Slater Steel Industries Ltd. IPSCO has 2000 employees. Its growth has paralleled the expansion of the oil-and-gas industry in Canada over the last twenty years, but its future depends on the rate and intensity of energy-resource development in Canada.

Native Metal Industries received start-up funds from the Province of Saskatchewan and the federal Department of Regional Economic Expansion (DREE) and operated on land financed by the Saskatchewan Economic Development Corporation (SEDCO). IPSCO provides NMI with the raw materials necessary to carry out its operations: it supplies NMI with old boxcars that are stripped by NMI workers, while the remaining steel is cut into sheets measuring approximately sixty centimetres by ninety centimetres; these are returned to IPSCO for use in the furnaces that feed their steel mill, and NMI is paid according to the number of tonnes of steel it has cut. If IPSCO workers are on strike, NMI must shut down; if IPSCO runs out of used boxcars, NMI must suspend its operations until a new shipment is provided. In the mid-1970s, NMI was in financial difficulty, and it received additional funds from the Saskatchewan Department of Industry and Commerce and the Department of Indian and Northern Affairs; IPSCO provided a new parcel of land about 1.5 kilometres from the IPSCO site.

The shareholders of NMI are its employees, and they are all of Indian ancestry. Since NMI is basically a training industry, some of its employees eventually move on to jobs with IPSCO. Many NMI employees prefer, however, to remain with NMI once their training is completed. A representative of IPSCO is on NMI's Board of Directors.

This case-study differs from the others in that it consists in the analysis of a company which constitutes, in effect, a training program, rather than in the analysis of a program that is one of a company's many divisions. For this reason, at NMI it was possible to interview the two senior managers and seven of the nine members of the Board of Directors.

The NMI Native Program

History

From 1970 to 1976

In the early 1970s, the Premier of Saskatchewan set up a task force to identify economic opportunities available to people of Indian ancestry. The task force consisted of businessmen, government representatives, and Native leaders. Their meetings did not produce immediate results, but one member eventually suggested a scheme to create employment for Native people on a long-term basis: this member was then president of IPSCO and knew that his company could purchase old boxcars from the United States, transport them into Canada, dismantle them, and use the scrap-iron to feed the furnaces of its steel mill. IPSCO could have handled all phases of this operation, but the president was convinced that the steel-cutting phase was an opportunity to establish a separate small industry that could be run by Native people.

Following meetings between senior IPSCO management and representatives of the Governments of Saskatchewan and Canada, a proposal was drawn up to create Native Metal Industries, a company that would employ and train Native people in Regina. Initial funding was provided by the Government of Saskatchewan and DREE in the amount of $100 000. IPSCO provided raw materials, as well as technical and managerial expertise. The original intent was that all NMI employees would be of Indian ancestry; half of these employees would be Treaty Indian, and half would be Métis; the group would wholly own the company.

The following five organizations participated in the establishment of Native Metal Industries and were represented on the NMI Board of Directors: IPSCO, the Federation of Saskatchewan Indians (FSI), the Métis Society of Saskatchewan, the federal Department of Indian Affairs and Northern Development (DIAND), and the Saskatchewan Department of Indian Affairs (now defunct). The president of NMI was also chairman of its Board of Directors and vice-president of FSI. Representatives from government and business and four NMI employees made up the other members of the NMI Board.

The five organizations mentioned above recruited the first twenty employees of NMI, but the Board rapidly became ineffective when a power struggle developed between employees who were affiliated either with the FSI or with the Métis Society. In its first five years, NMI was highly politicized, and outside advisers severed their ties with the organization as a result of pressure from Native groups. Internal management was untrained, could not give employees appropriate direction and training, did not keep proper accounting records or personnel files, hired too many men for the number of jobs available, overpaid employees, and placed more emphasis on social activities, such as company-sponsored sports teams and life-skills courses, than on on-the-job training. The results were disastrous: absenteeism and staff turnover were extremely high; employees were unskilled, untrained, and unfamiliar with an industrial setting; equipment was mishandled and rendered unusable; accounts payable were ignored; loans and advances to employees were seldom repaid; and the company shares were owned by a small number of individuals. Nevertheless, financial statements reflected moderate profits, and it was not until mid-1976 that outsiders became aware that the company was on the verge of bankruptcy. By that time the political strife had been ironed out, and some employees had managed to keep the company afloat, but the financial situation was so poor that they had to ask for external assistance.

In the fall of 1976, a task force, consisting of representatives of the Saskatchewan Department of Industry and Commerce, Native Metal Industries, the Royal Bank of Canada, SEDCO, and IPSCO, was set up to consider ways of saving NMI from bankruptcy. The task force concluded that an investment of at least $250 000 would be required to get NMI back on its feet, and that definite steps would have to be taken, such as acquiring the necessary financial backing and persuading creditors to be patient during NMI's recovery period.

The federal Department of Indian Affairs and Northern Development and the Saskatchewan Department of Industry and

Commerce agreed to give NMI a new start by granting it $150 000 and $100 000 respectively.   The Saskatchewan contribution was a grant from the "Economic Development Program for Disadvantaged Persons", made to enable "Native Metal Industries Ltd. to remain in operation until long-range and complete financing could be arranged."[1]   An agreement was signed, on 2 December 1976, between the Minister of the Saskatchewan Department of Industry and Commerce and Native Metal Industries; some of its stipulations are of particular interest. Native Metal Industries was required thereafter to:

- Report to Saskatchewan's Minister of Industry and Commerce
- Restructure its Board of Directors to include four employees elected by its shareholders, one representative of the federal Department of Indian Affairs, one from the provincial Department of Industry and Commerce, one from IPSCO, and two business men appointed by the other directors
- Employ a mix of 100 Indian and Métis persons
- Appoint a general manager, a production manager, and a consulting manager
- Offer training to its employees
- Reinvest its profits in the company
- Maintain proper accounting records
- Identify the employees "social, cultural, recreational and welfare needs and arrange for funding...."[2]

From 1976 to 1980

Though NMI had functioned informally until December 1976, it began to assume a very definite corporate structure in early 1977: a new Board of Directors was struck, and it immediately began to implement some of the conditions of the December 1976 agreement. The Board hired a consulting manager who was a specialist in labour negotiations, but who had never worked with Native people. His mandate was to assist NMI in achieving financial stability and to train employees to run their company as a business. A general manager was also named by the Board, and he was responsible for overall production; he had been working with NMI for many years and was familiar with all aspects of this area. These persons, who both reported to the Board, began to run the company as a team. Reporting to the general manager were: a senior foreman, a safety foreman, and an administrative supervisor. Technically, no one reported to the consulting manager, but since he was the only person who provided administrative and financial training to all employees, as, if, and when required, he had some control over the operation of the company.

Within one year of the initiation of these arrangements, NMI had made an amazing recovery. It had achieved a net income of $130 000 and had reversed its financial situation: a negative working capital of $160 000 at the end of 1976 had become a positive working capital of $20 000 by the end of 1977. From 1977 to 1980, financial stability had been achieved, employee turnover had diminished, equipment was in good order, employees received better training, and productivity had increased. Moreover an incentive scheme was created whereby employees can earn higher wages if they increase their productivity and, if they remain with the company for at least a year, they can become shareholders.

Objectives

Native Metal Industries Ltd. was created in 1970 as a training centre for Native people who, after they had worked for NMI, would be better qualified to find a job in industry. IPSCO management, government representatives, and Native leaders recognized that not enough jobs were available to meet the demand for work caused by the influx of Native people into Regina. Furthermore these migrants were not prepared for existing jobs, either because of a lack of education or because of a lack of training, or for both reasons.

NMI's first objective is to provide training and employment to people of Indian ancestry who have not previously worked in an industrial setting or in a large city, and who would find it difficult to secure employment with other companies. NMI can be described as a 'sheltered workshop', where a Native person can learn what to expect from an industrial setting and is allowed time to adjust, without having to cope with the pressure of losing his job if he does not quickly measure up to expectations. It also permits the Native person to continue living on his reserve. In fact, many workers commute 200 kilometres a day because they prefer to live on their reserves.

The philosophy underlying the NMI concept is that, through various incentives, an employee will be motivated to better his condition and to consider steady employment, rather than to rely on temporary or occasional jobs. The program's founders believed that the development of new aspirations in the Native worker would lead to an improvement of his status in the market-place. Moreover they assumed that Indians are better equipped to deal with Indians than are persons of widely different ethnic and socio-cultural backgrounds, and that an Indian-run company could be successful. Many similar attempts have been failures in the past, but NMI survived, perhaps because many individuals shared this belief and worked together to bring it to reality.

Implementation and Functioning

With the reorganization of NMI in early 1977, considerable changes were also made on the production side. The number of employees dropped from approximately one hundred and twenty in 1975, to seventy in 1980, but the company's net production increased. Employees were better trained, required less supervision, and became better motivated as they witnessed the recovery of the company. Because the number of jobs NMI has to offer is limited, and because employees' productivity is always on the increase, employees realize that they are in a competitive situation and, therefore, must accept company rules more readily than they did in the past.

In the post-1976 period, NMI adopted two incentives designed to increase productivity. The first provided employees with an opportunity to increase their earnings. Since it was estimated that the normal daily output for one man is ten tonnes of cut steel, a worker who produces more than that amount per day is paid an additional number of dollars per additional tonne. The second incentive, which had existed before the 1976 agreement discontinued it, was reinstated under new conditions. Earlier employees had been given the option of becoming shareholders in the company. Originally they had access to class-A preferred shares, which they could purchase after two years' service; the purchase entitled them to a share in company ownership and participation in profits. Class-A shares, which were valued at $1815 in 1975, could be purchased through payroll deduction. Class-B shares were also available at a cost of $1.00 each to class-A shareholders, as well as to employees with less than two years of service. Class-B shares did not offer a share in ownership, but gave their purchasers the right to vote on matters of company policy. Because of high employee turnover, Class-A shares were in the hands of only two employees at the time of the 1976 breakdown, and nine employees owned class-B shares.

The 1976 agreement stipulates that employees are entitled to buy one share of stock after one year of service and an additional share after each ensuing year. At present, thirty-four shareholders own a total of one hundred shares, yet they have no knowledge of the net worth of the company. According to the 1976 agreement, shareholders are not to receive dividends. If and when profits are made, the money must be reinvested in the company. 'Employee ownership' of Native Metal

Industries is rather symbolic, yet every employee who was eligible to be a shareholder had become one, though he was under no obligation to do so.

Criteria of Eligibility for Personnel Recruitment

Recruits for NMI must be of Indian ancestry, in good health, since the work is physically demanding, and interested in working as steel cutters or heavy equipment operators. There are no requirements or limitations pertaining to age, sex or education.

Methods of recruitment

NMI has never had to recruit actively. As soon as word gets out that jobs are available, applicants appear in droves. The Métis Society in Regina and Canada Manpower Centres in Saskatchewan frequently refer candidates to NMI.

Union involvement

NMI workers formed an intra-plant union in 1972, which functioned informally for five years. Though it lacked structure, it taught workers to negotiate for their rights and thereby improve their working conditions. The general manager, while he was president of the NMI union from 1973 to 1976, became acquainted with a United Steelworkers' representative who worked at IPSCO. The two men had many discussions about the ways in which a formal union would improve the working conditions of NMI employees. However, the IPSCO union representative became formally involved with NMI only when his assistance was requested at the end of 1976. With the technical assistance of the consulting manager, NMI became a separate local of United Steelworkers in January 1977.

Indicators of Employee Adaptation

Employee turnover

From 1970 to 1980, over 1000 Native people worked for NMI. A study carried out in 1979 indicated that 300 of these people were permanently employed elsewhere. Of the others, some were still working at NMI, some had returned to their reserves, and others could not be traced. Of the sixty or seventy employees currently at NMI, thirty-four have been with the company for a least four years and three of these have been there for ten years; the rest had joined the company within the preceding year.

Many factors explain the high turnover of employees during the first six years of NMI's operation; some of these factors were mentioned earlier. In addition, some employees left NMI because they could not adapt to a regular forty-hour-a-week job; others were terminated or left because of a particular social problem; others could not cope with a highly politicized environment; still others left to take better jobs, or because they did not want to work as steel cutters. Some employees left and returned to NMI several times. The incentive scheme, whereby a worker is paid extra money if he produces more than the normal daily quota, improved worker stability. Today it is estimated that at least 70 per cent of NMI's labour force is stable, whereas in the early years, this figure stood at about 10 per cent.

Absenteeism

Absenteeism was a serious problem in the first half of the 1970s. Managers never knew, from day to day, how many of their workers would arrive at the job. NMI found it necessary to hire more workers than were actually needed to carry out the daily work-load. For example, fifty workers would be hired to do the job of thirty in order to ensure that daily productivity standards were met. Occasionally the company would send a bus around to neighbouring reserves to pick up workers in order to make sure of enough manpower to get a job done.

Since 1978, however, employees who do not arrive at work on a given day are not paid for that day, and they are terminated after two days of unexplained absence. Though absenteeism still occurs, these deterrents have reduced it considerably.

Productivity

NMI managers believe that improvements in productivity paralleled a decrease in employee turnover both because of the work-incentive scheme and because workers were enjoying the benefits of steady employment. When the company was formed, a worker was expected to cut six and a half tonnes of steel per day. Over time, this figure rose to ten tonnes. In fact, the daily output in 1980 averaged thirteen and a half to fourteen tonnes per man. The workers were better trained and were always inventing new techniques to increase productivity. If the material were available, every man could cut a least one boxcar per day (that is, eighteen to twenty tonnes of steel), and some workers are able to process as much as twenty-seven to thirty-six tonnes a day.

Conclusions

Let us review some of the characteristics of Native Metal industries from the perspective of an on-the-job training program.

Equality

Native Metal Industries is committed to treating all its employees alike. Since its employees are all Native, Native versus non-Native discrimination is not an issue. However, NMI tries to assure a balance among its Native staff: half of its employees are status Indians, and half are non-status Indians and Métis.

Government Participation

NMI has been heavily subsidized by governments: it received grants of $100 000 in 1970 and $250 000 in 1976. Board members are trying to erase the impression that NMI is merely a government-subsidy program, but if they decide to diversify, government grants will be solicited for a third time. The Governments of Canada and Saskatchewan are represented on the NMI Board of Directors, and NMI can take no major financial decision without their permission. The December 1976 agreement that NMI signed puts government in full control of the company's operations.

Corporate Support

IPSCO provides NMI with materials and, on an occasional basis, with technical and managerial expertise. IPSCO representatives sit on NMI's Board, but IPSCO does not appear to play as active a role in NMI affairs as the Saskatchewan Power Corporation plays in supporting the Headstart Employment Corporation.

Native Participation

NMI was entirely run and staffed by Native people until the end of 1976. The non-Native people on NMI's original Board were not able to carry out their roles effectively because of Native politics at the time. Today the company is said to be Native-run and Native-owned. However, the company is actually under the control of a Board of Directors and is accountable to the Saskatchewan Minister of Industry and Commerce. The consulting manager is non-Native, and he makes all the day-to-day financial decisions. The shareholders do not receive profits and, if profits are made, they must be reinvested in the company. The Board members, four of whom are non-Native, make all the major financial decisions, and the shareholders (employees) are unaware of the worth of the company. If the company is dissolved, whatever moneys are left must be returned to the government. The assumption on which NMI was built is that Indians are better equipped to deal with Indians than are non-Natives, but this belief, as events have shown, must be tempered by the reality that without appropriate business training and experience, it is impossible to run a successful enterprise.

Native Adaptation

The 1976 agreement stipulated that the NMI Board "take steps to identify the social, cultural, recreational, and welfare needs of employees, and to arrange for funding of same." No evidence of such activity appeared during the interviews, except for a reference to a life-skills seminar held twice a year. Although adaptation to mainstream society may be a goal for NMI as a thriving corporate entity, it cannot occur if its workers continue to be isolated from the reality of other industrial environments. Life-skills training would assist workers to adapt to other environments if they wished and would provide them with more employment opportunities.

In conclusion, we have observed many similarities between the Headstart and Native Metal Industries programs. It will be interesting to learn subsequently if these similarities are peculiar to the Province of Saskatchewan, where the government has demonstrated a willingness to stimulate the employment of people of Indian ancestry.

Notes

1. Agreement between the Minister of the Department of Industry and Commerce and Native Metal Industries Ltd., signed on 2 December 1976, Article 1.

2. *Ibid.*, Article 7. 6.

4: Syncrude Canada Limited

Characteristics and Setting

Syncrude Canada Limited is a Canadian-owned consortium involved in the production of synthetic crude oil in the Athabasca Tar Sands at Mildred Lake, 480 kilometres north of Edmonton. The oil is referred to as 'synthetic' because it is entrapped in bituminous sands resembling asphalt, from which it must be extracted before undergoing a series of refining processes that will liquefy it and render it suitable for pipeline transmission.

There are 3000 employees at Syncrude, 9 per cent of whom are of Indian ancestry. The majority of employees live in the town of Fort McMurray, situated at the confluence of the Athabasca and Clearwater Rivers, fifty kilometres from the Syncrude plant. The population of Fort McMurray grew from 1000 residents in 1960 to 24 000 in 1981. The original inhabitants of the town and its surrounding areas were mostly of Indian ancestry.

A unique feature of the Syncrude case-study is that the company has set up a separate department to manage a variety of Native

programs, and that department is amost entirely staffed by Native
people. Figures given for the number of Native workers in Syncrude
varied from 200 to 285.

The Native Development Program

History

Syncrude's Native development program evolved in three phases. In this
section, we shall look at the events that characterized the first two
phases: the planning phase (1972/1975), and the construction phase
(1975/1978). The third phase, production (1978 and on), will be given
detailed attention in the following section.

Planning phase

Though Syncrude was not officially established until 1972, the concept had
been on the drawing-board for twelve years. During that period, the
shareholders named a president who, in collaboration with a Board of
Directors, drafted three consecutive applications requesting permission
from the Alberta government to develop the tar sands. Meanwhile the
Government of Alberta began to promote the policy that local people
should be hired preferentially in new industrial enterprises in north-
eastern Alberta. Syncrude and Bechtel Canada, the project's managing
contractor in 1972, were equally committed to hiring local residents; in
this case, that meant hiring people of Indian ancestry.

When Syncrude entered its active planning phase in 1972, leaders of
the Indian Association of Alberta and of the Alberta Métis Association
began pressuring senior government officials to guarantee that Native
people would be employed in this major project. Syncrude management,
particularly because of the influence of their president, wanted to involve
Native people from the start; in 1973 they formalized their commitment

in a position paper entitled "Employment of Residents of Northeastern Alberta." The paper stipulates that Syncrude will hire residents of north-eastern Alberta, train them if necessary, and try to stimulate the involvement of other industries, governments, and Native people in similar undertakings.[1] The position paper leads the reader to assume that Native people were the target population, since they constituted the majority of residents in north-eastern Alberta. The paper states that these Northerners were underqualified for industrial employment, and that many of them were unprepared for urban living. The paper was widely distributed to Syncrude employees, government employment agencies, Native groups, and contractors. It set forth Syncrude's policy on the employment of Native people and augured well for future working arrangements.

In 1974 Syncrude set up a Community Relations Division under its Public Affairs Department and hired two Native residents of Fort McMurray to make it operational, to create links with the various Native associations and bands, and to assist in the recruitment of Native people who would work for Bechtel Canada at the Syncrude construction site.

During the same period, Native Outreach, which was funded by Canada Manpower and Immigration, set up offices in Fort McMurray to inform Native people of employment and training opportunities in north-eastern Alberta. Recruitment activities were brought to a halt for a two-month period when the Atlantic Richfield Company (ARCO) pulled out of the Syncrude consortium in December 1974.

Construction phase

Construction got under way at Syncrude on 3 February 1975, when the Governments of Canada, Alberta and Ontario provided the necessary equity to replace ARCO's contribution. During the four-year period of construction, Bechtel hired 8000 people, 800 of whom were of Indian ancestry. These figures apply to a peak period, but the average number of construction workers of Indian ancestry over the entire period was 550.

Bechtel's two Native recruiters worked with the Construction and General Workers Union, Native Outreach, and Keyano College, a vocational training centre located in Fort McMurray. Bechtel made arrangements with Keyano College to design and offer a course that prepared Native people to work in an industrial milieu. Six hundred Native people were referred to Keyano College for a five-week Industrial Workers Course, and 540 of them were subsequently hired by Bechtel to work at Mildred Lake. As one researcher has pointed out in a study of Native integration in Fort McMurray, Bechtel officials were successful in hiring Native people because "they maintained an open-door policy at the camp, encouraging local native community leaders to visit. In return, the company officials visited the communities in an attempt to influence local people to work for them."[2]

In 1975 Syncrude hired a Native-development co-ordinator, who worked in the Employee Relations Division. His mandate was to draw up a proposal outlining the nature and content of what was to be Syncrude's package of Native programs. The co-ordinator, who is a Cree Indian, consulted Americans and Canadians who were running Native programs in the private sector and met regularly with a group of Syncrude representatives in order to develop a comprehensive Native program. As a result of his investigation, he submitted a document on 31 December 1975, entitled "An Action Plan for Native Training and Counselling Programs". This plan served as a framework to establish Syncrude's Native Development Department.

The Action Plan

The Action Plan suggests that Syncrude develop its Native programs in three areas: life skills, family counselling, and social and cultural training[3].   Life-skills and family-counselling programs should be designed to assist the worker and his family to adapt to urban living and should include assistance in finding suitable housing, in managing a household, in placing children in appropriate schools, in financial planning, in coping with isolation from the family's reserve, and, generally, in integrating the Native family into all aspects of urban community life. The cultural training program was intended to give Native workers a forum to discuss problems related to their work environment. Further, it was recommended that two Native people experienced in social work, curriculum development, and cultural exchange programs, be hired to work with the Native co-ordinator, to put such services into place before the first group of Native workers was taken on. It was also suggested that a training program focusing on Native culture be developed for Syncrude supervisors.

The Plan recommends that Native trainees have completed a minimum of Grade-10 education and, if they have not, that they be given a letter of intent to hire, which guarantees them a job once they have accomplished the necessary academic upgrading. It also suggests that Syncrude work with Alberta vocational colleges to design training programs for Native people who would be prospective employees, and that it develop contacts with Indian band councils, Métis settlement councils, Native Outreach, reserves, local communities, high schools, and the news media in order to increase the number of Native recruits.

Syncrude approved the Action Plan, and implementation began in early 1976. A family counsellor and a Native cultural instructor were hired to set up Native Training and Counselling Programs; they also worked with the two Native employees who started up the Community Affairs Division in 1974.

The Indian Opportunities Agreement

After the Action Plan had been approved, an agreement, referred to as the 'Syndcrude Indian Opportunities Agreement', was signed on 3 July 1976 by Syncrude Canada Limited, the federal government, and the Indian Association of Alberta. This agreement formalized some of the recommendations of the Action Plan and specified the nature of the role of each participant. It was impossible to determine why this agreement was produced at that particular time; one can only speculate that pressure may have been exerted by the Indian Association, and that the federal government wanted to have a higher profile in Syncrude's activities, since it had recently become a shareholder. Though the Indian Opportunities Agreement refers only to Treaty Indians, Syncrude has interpreted its terms as applicable to all persons of Indian ancestry.

Syncrude's role. Syncrude agreed to recruit Treaty Indians with required skills, to offer letters of intent to those who were willing to upgrade their education in vocational schools, "to publicize opportunities for Treaty Indians...to investigate complaints of discrimination...to offer counselling to Indian employees and their families...to monitor the Indian employee's performance and assist in his career progression."[4]

The federal government's role. The federal government agreed to publicize jobs available at Syncrude, to fund academic upgrading and life-skills courses for Native people wishing to work at Syncrude, and to set up and fund the Indian Oil Sands Economic Development Corporation and the Indian Equity Fund, in order to promote the creation of Indian businesses in the Tar Sands region.

The role of the Indian Association of Alberta. The Indian Association of Alberta (IAA) agreed to "assist in publicizing job openings, assist Indian students to remain in training programs, and evaluate the success of training and request alternative programs if necessary."[5]

Objectives

Syncrude's original objective was to hire residents of north-eastern Alberta, most of whom were of Indian ancestry, for the construction and production phases of its operation. In 1976 Syncrude began to offer employment to Indians from all parts of Alberta and to support and promote actively Indian-owned businesses in the Tar Sands region. However, by the end of its construction phase, in mid-1978, the number of Native employees at Syncrude had dropped dramatically. For many of them, it was difficult to make the transition from the construction phase to the production phase. At this point Syncrude reaffirmed its commitment to hire local Native labour by creating a Department of Native Development Programs. The department's mandate is to meet three objectives:

- To help Native people realize their full employment potential
- To educate non-Native Syncrude employees about the cultural background of Native people
- To assist Native businessmen in the area.

Implementation and Functioning

In late 1977 Syncrude hired a Native person as supervisor of Manpower Planning. In 1978 he formed the Department of Native Development Programs, which brought together the supervisor of Manpower Planning, the two Native recruiters who had set up the Community Relations Division in 1974, and the family counsellor and the cultural instructor hired in 1976 to set up Native Training and Counselling Programs. The new department's first task was to draw up a five-year plan outlining its objectives, the package of programs it would offer, and the nature of the new policies that Syncrude would be required to adopt in order to accomplish these goals. The department also launched an informal, in-house, educational campaign whereby managers of departments were informed of the objectives and programs relating to Native people that Syncrude had endorsed: the managers' assistance was solicited to ensure that all employees become familiar with these changes.

The implementation of the Native Development Programs was a two-year incremental process that involved, by the end of 1980, administration staff in the following twelve positions: a senior program co-ordinator; a co-ordinator of community and business development; a business-development co-ordinator; a supervisor of recruitment and family counselling, who is also a Native-liaison officer; two family counsellors; a Native recruiter; two job counsellors; a Native-training supervisor and two support staff. Eleven of these positions were held by Native people, eight of whom were interviewed for this study; it was not possible, however, to interview Native employees, who are the clientèle of the Native Development Program.

The Department of Native Development

The Department of Native Development includes two divisions: Native Programs, and Community and Business Development. The former facilitates the integration of Native workers and their families into the labour force and into the community; the latter offers a variety of support services to Native entrepreneurs. The department is run by a senior program co-ordinator who is responsible for program planning and liaison with Syncrude's senior management.

Native Programs Division

The main functions of this division include recruitment, advising employees on job-related matters, and family counselling. These duties are carried out by a staff of five persons, under the direction of a supervisor who, in addition, acts as liaison officer between Syncrude and Native communities and educational institutions in Alberta, and who organizes Information Workshops and Career Opportunities Seminars.

Job advisers. Syncrude's two Native job advisers are responsible for trying to solve problems, both technical and interpersonal, which may occur at the work site. Their goal is to find a solution for problems before they escalate into major issues.

Native recruiters. A Native recruiter is responsible for informing Native people of job openings, and for ensuring that they have an opportunity to apply. The recruiter, who screens and hires all Native candidates, works in collaboration with the Employee Relations Department, as well as with the Native-job advisers and Native family counsellors. He maintains external contacts with Native Outreach, Canada Manpower Centres, local Indian band councils, Native communities, and with high schools and vocational schools as well.

The most basic criterion for employment at Syncrude is that a candidate demonstrate a willingness to learn. Grade-10 standing in English, mathematics and science, as well as good health are prerequisites for permanent employment. Exceptions in the matter of academic standing are sometimes made for candidates with a sound work history in a particular job category. Other candidates who appear promising, but who lack the required educational background, are encouraged to upgrade their education and are given guidance on how to accomplish this.

Family counsellors. This position was created in 1976; there are now two family counsellors at Syncrude. They offer pre-employment counselling, which consists of meeting the employee and his family before they move to Fort McMurray, to determine their particular needs. Syncrude offers a Relocation Service to all its employees. The service consists of a housing program administered by Northward Developments, which includes 1000 houses, town houses, and apartments built for Syncrude employees. When Syncrude hires an employee, Northward representatives take him on a tour of available housing units. Once he has chosen his accommodation, Northward advises the family counsellors of his expected date of arrival. When the family has settled in, the family counsellors contact it again, take the family on a tour of the city, help the parents register their children in school, and introduce them to the Native Friendship Centre and other social centres. For the next three months, the counsellors visit the families every three weeks to offer advice in matters of budgeting, banking, availability of social, health, and recreational services, shopping facilities, and whatever is required to facilitate their adaptation to an urban environment. Families who have been established for three to six months are visited monthly; after a year, biannual visits are made. Some Native families refuse the services of family consellors, but most accept them.

The counsellors reported that they had no difficulty in communicating with Native families because they both spoke a Native language, had lived on a reserve themselves, and knew all the families. They worked in collaboration with the Native Friendship Centre, Native Counselling Services of Alberta, the Alcohol and Drug Abuse Centre, and the Department of Consumer Affairs.

Cultural Instructor. The Cultural Instructor, formerly the Social Relations Instructor, gives two, one-day, Cultural Awareness Seminars each month to Syncrude employees to expand their knowledge of Native culture. Native-job advisers participate in these sessions. A parallel seminar is also offered to Native employees. Both these seminars are meant to develop a mutual understanding of different attitudes and behaviour, to eliminate stereotyping, and to improve working relationships.

Community and Business Development Division
A senior co-ordinator is responsible to ensure that business opportunities

for Native people are maximized within Syncrude and within the surrounding community, and that the aims and objectives of the Indian Oil Sands Economic Development Corporation and the Indian Equity Fund are respected. Another co-ordinator provides direct assistance to Native businesses. This assistance includes market studies, feasibility studies, contract arrangements, financial advice, and tendering for the supply of goods and services to Syncrude.

The Department of Native Development offers a variety of programs and services, including the following:

Mining-Trainees Program. Teams of eight Native trainees are hired for a two-month probationary period. During this time they are exposed to the different types of jobs required for open-pit mining. If they are interested in this type of work, they can exercise their option to become permanent employees.

Rotation Program. This program was designed to permit Native people to be permanently employed while continuing to live in their own community. Fourteen employees are flown into Fort McMurray from Fort Chippewan for a seven-day work shift. Syncrude lodges these men on their campsite for seven days and then flies them back to Fort Chippewan, where they remain with their families for seven days. At the same time, Syncrude pilots pick up a second crew from Fort Chippewan and fly it to the Syncrude site for another seven days. Two crews rotate to fill the jobs of one crew at all times.

Social Adaptation Program. This program is still at the design stage. It will focus on spouses of workers and will try to provide means to alleviate the problems of their isolation and loneliness in the city.

Native Secretarial Training Program. This program provides on-the-job training for Native women who wish to acquire secretarial skills.

Native Summer Students' Work Program. High school students are selected by Syncrude's Native-liaison officer during visits to various schools in Alberta throughout the year and are offered summer employment.

Native Student Awards Program. Twenty Native students from Grades 8 and 9 are awarded a small amount of money at the end of the school year on the basis of their academic performance as an encouragement to continue their studies.

Native Scholarship Fund. Four students each year receive a scholarship to attend university and are assured a summer job for the duration of their undergraduate studies.

Indicators of Adaptation

Employee turnover

For the years 1978, 1979 and 1980, Native-employee turnover was respectively 60, 44 and 30 per cent. For the years 1979 and 1980, there was no significant difference between Native and non-Native-employee turnover. Some observers remarked that Native-employee turnover stabilized as a result of the creation of the Department of Native Development and of the impact of the Cultural-Awareness Seminars.

Absenteeism

Absenteeism was a serious problem for Native workers at Syncrude, but seems to be less pronounced since the positions of family and job counsellors were created in 1976. When an employee is absent, counsellors telephone his home to enquire the reason; if there is a problem, they offer to visit the family to suggest ways of solving it. If the problem relates to alcoholism, the employee is referred to a rehabilitation centre.

Productivity

Most respondents believed that there was no difference between the productivity of the Native worker and that of the non-Native worker. One respondent, however, claimed that Native productivity was higher, but since no objective tests were available, this observation could not be verified.

Conclusions

The thrust and support of Syncrude's Native employment practices originated in the work of its first president and, to this day, senior management is committed to the maintenance and development of Native programs. The Native Development Department seems to offer the most comprehensive package of programs and services available to Native employees anywhere in Canada. It is unique in that it was initiated and implemented almost exclusively by persons of Indian ancestry. The creators of this department were guided by the belief that not just one, but a variety of programs and services would be necessary to accommodate the different categories of Native employees, and that these programs and services should be designed incrementally, that is, as needs were identified.

The basic philosophy of the Department of Native Development is that education is the great equalizer, that it starts in the community, and that both Native and non-Native people have a responsibility in this regard. This is why many Syncrude programs are designed to impress upon young people the value of education and to reach out to and involve Native communities. Syncrude recognizes that once Native people become part of the work environment, that environment must change to facilitate their adaptation. It does not assume that only the Native person must change to fit the industrial *milieu*. Conversely, it has created an atmosphere where non-Native employees can acquire an awareness and an understanding of the Native person and accept that non-Natives, too, must change. This is the premise on which the cultural awareness seminars are built.

The Syncrude example is also outstanding in that as far back as 1975, a systematic investigation was undertaken of what was being done elsewhere. The Department of Native Development does, indeed, reflect the orientation of the 1975 Action Plan and the 1976 Indian Opportunity Agreement.

With respect to the promotion of Native businesses in the Tar Sands region, Syncrude acknowledges that if an industry settles in a particular area, it should not only hire local workers, but it should also ensure that local entrepreneurs benefit from its presence. On this basis, Syncrude created the Indian Oil Sands Economic Development Corporation and the Indian Equity Fund, which provide financial assistance and support to Native entrepreneurs.

Notes

1. Syncrude Canada Limited, *Employment of Residents of Northeastern Alberta* 1973.

2. Kathy Littlejohn and Rick Powell, *A Study of Native Integration into the Fort McMurray Labour Force* (1980), for the Alberta Oil Sands Environmental Research Program by the Canadian Institute for Research in the Behavioural and Social Sciences.

3. Herb Callihoe, *An Action Plan for Native Training and Counselling Programs* (Syncrude Canada Limited 1975).

4. *Syncrude Indian Opportunities Agreement,* an agreement between the Department of Indian Affairs and Northern Development, Syncrude Canada Limited, and the Indian Association of Alberta, 3 July 1976.

5.   *Ibid.*

6.   The information in this section was gathered from two sources: interviews with Syncrude employees and a Syncrude publication entitled *Supervisors Handbook on Native Development Program* (September 1979).

5: NOVA, an Alberta Corporation

Characteristics and Setting

NOVA, an Alberta Corporation, formerly known as the 'Alberta Gas Trunk Line Company Limited' (AGTL), is a Canadian-owned diversified organization that operates nationally and internationally. NOVA consists of four major divisions: the Petrochemical Division, the Petroleum Division, the Manufacturing Division and the Pipeline Development Division.

NOVA employs 2079 persons in its Gas Transmission Division and its wholly owned subsidiaries, and 3290 persons in its partially owned subsidiaries and affiliates. There are approximately 1200 employees working for NOVA's Gas Transmission Division, seventy-seven of whom are of Indian ancestry.

In this chapter, we shall explore NOVA's Native Employment Program and its Opportunity Measures Plan. The former operates through the Human Resources Department of NOVA's Gas Transmission Division, the latter through the Alaska Project Division, a component of the Pipeline Development Division.

NOVA's Native Employment Program

History

When AGTL began to operate in the Yukon and Northwest Territories in
the early 1970s, its president observed that local Native people were not
involved in the company's operations and decided that this situation should
be rectified. As a result, AGTL lent its support, in 1973, to NORTRAN,[1]
a seven-company consortium set up to assist private petroleum-based
firms to plan employment strategies for Native people and to prepare
those people to function in an urban environment.

The consortium dissolved in 1976, when one of the participating
companies closed its doors, but NORTRAN continues to operate as a
private firm, offering counselling, recruitment and supervisory services to
private oil companies. Since AGTL was expecting to build the Foothills
pipeline in the Yukon, it developed the AGTL Foothills Training Program,
through which NORTRAN trained thirty-four Native northerners for
operation and maintenance jobs related to the construction phase of the
project. Since the beginning of this phase was postponed, AGTL absorbed
the Foothills trainees into its Gas Transmission Division.

The second significant indication of AGTL's commitment to hiring
Native people was the release of a statement by the president, in July
1976, recommending the creation of a Native-employment program
specifically tailored to meet AGTL's manpower needs. A Native-
employment officer was hired in that same year to ensure that the
percentage of Native employees in AGTL be at least the same as the
percentage of Native people resident in Alberta, that is, 5 per cent.

The next major development in Native employment was AGTL's
involvement, in 1978, with a specialized training program at the Alberta
Vocational Centre located in the village of Grouard near Lesser Slave
Lake (AVC-Grouard). This program was developed to provide job training

and life skills to Native northerners who would eventually be hired for the construction phase of the Alaska gas pipeline. Since the pipeline would be crossing many Alberta reserves, it was taken for granted that Native people should have access to, and be prepared for, the approximately 2500 jobs that the pipeline construction would create.

Objectives

According to four respondents in senior positions at NOVA, AGTL's desire to employ Native northerners was founded on the conviction that it makes good business sense to hire Native people because of their competence, and that a company has the moral obligation to offer employment opportunities to all persons living in the area of its operations. For these reasons, NOVA continues to hire Native people, though it reached its 5 per cent objective in 1980. One respondent remarked that the trend to develop Native-employment programs was initially a response to government pressure and to growing recognition of corporate responsibility, but that in the 1980s, the trend is to maximize the growth of human resources. He stated that because there is a great demand for a variety of skills, companies should not overlook the potential contribution of one minority group or another.

Another trend that began in the United States and is now apparent in most provinces, except for Alberta and Quebec, is the proliferation of Affirmative Action Programs. Though Affirmative Action was ruled illegal in Alberta courts because of the supremacy those courts accorded to human rights legislation, NOVA nevertheless joined this trend by making special efforts to increase the numbers of Natives, women and handicapped persons on its staff. NOVA managers refer to programs intended to develop the human resource as 'Positive Action' rather than 'Affirmative Action'; they consider that the latter term tends to create more barriers and more bureaucracy than are desirable.

As one respondent commented, "Quota systems that are not performance-oriented defeat the purpose for which they were established. Numbers cannot be sustained if individuals are forced to quit because of insufficient job preparation."

To recognize human potential and to match it with the company's needs seems to be the *modus operandi* of NOVA's Native-employment program. The focus is on what a person can do rather than on his or her level of education and experience. One respondent stated that ideally, NOVA's Native recruiter tries to learn what motivates a candidate and the extent of his or her potential, and then to match this person to an appropriate job, maximize his or her opportunities for training, and allow him or her time to adjust and develop, while monitoring on-the-job performance and offering career counselling as needed.

Implementation and Functioning

Native Employment Program

From 1976 to 1978, NOVA hired consecutively two Native recruitment officers to implement its Native Employment Program, but these officers are no longer with the company. A third Native recruitment officer, hired in 1978, was available for an interview. When he accepted his position, he tried to find out why AGTL had not attracted more Native people. He learned that information about available jobs seldom reached Native potential employees and, when it did, job requirements did not match their particular skills. He proceeded to build a network of possible sources of Native recruitment and to carry out an in-house survey to discover how many jobs would be available in each department, and how they could be restructured to accommodate Native people.

Native applicants are interviewed by the Native-recruitment co-ordinator, either during his visit to reserves or, in case of a referral, in his office. During the interview, the Native co-ordinator tries to determine the candidate's suitability for a particular job and informs him of the company's expectations. If the candidate seems promising, the co-ordinator discusses career-advancement opportunities within the company and the services available to Native people within the community where he will work. If a candidate is interested in training for a particular trade, he may write an apprenticeship entrance examination. The Native co-ordinator then checks the applicant's references. A last pre-employment step in the recruitment process is a visit to the work site, where the Native co-ordinator introduces the candidate to his prospective supervisor. A second interview takes place with the supervisor, who makes the final recommendation for employment. Candidates are asked to include their families in this visit, particularly if relocation is involved. The Native co-ordinator briefs the supervisor on the particular circumstances of the candidate and informs local agencies that their services may be called upon.

If there are no positions available at the time of the interview, the application is put on file, and the applicant is contacted three months later to see if he is still seeking employment. The role of the Native recruiter also includes counselling Native employees and monitoring their progress. Since 1978, the Native recruiter has also been involved in selecting Native trainees for the Basic Job Readiness Training and Life-Skills Program given at AVC-Grouard. This program will be discussed below. Since 1980 the position of the Native-recruitment officer has also incuded evaluations of socio-economic programs for Native people.

Criteria of eligibility. The person who has a good working background, who has been involved in a variety of activities, and who is not an alcoholic is the preferred candidate. He must also demonstrate to the recruiter that he is able and willing to train for a particular job. There is no minimum educational requirement.

Methods of recruitment. In order to recruit Native employees, links were created with Canada Manpower Centres in Alberta, the Indian Association of Alberta, Native Outreach, Indian News Media, the Federation of Métis Colonies, Friendship Centres, the Alberta Native Communications Society, band councils, employment counsellors on reserves, the Métis Association of Alberta, AGTL Native employees, high schools, vocational schools, and universities. Once job descriptions were rewritten, they were forwarded to these agencies, which soon began making referrals to AGTL as suitable candidates became available. Contacts were also made with AGTL's subsidiaries to inform them of the availability of Native candidates and to keep informed of their job openings.

Basic Job-Readiness Training and Life-Skills Program

The Grouard program of Basic Job-Readiness Training and Life-Skills was developed in 1978 by Foothills (Alberta), that is, AGTL, in collaboration with the federal government and the Government of Alberta. The federal government, through the Canada Employment and Immigration Commission, sponsors the courses, which cost about $3500 per trainee over a sixteen-week period. The Alberta Department of Advanced Education and Manpower provides the facilities at AVC-Grouard and assists in curriculum development; any direct contribution that the province makes is reimbursed by the federal government. NOVA provides advertising, recruitment, job placement, and follow-up counselling.

This program was developed on the grounds that the proposed construction of the Alaska Gas Pipeline would create 2000 jobs for Albertans, and it was considered right that Native northerners should have access to some of these opportunities. Since 1978, the program has been administered by three interrelated organizations: AGTL (now NOVA), Foothills (Alberta), and the Alaska Project Division (APD).

AVC-Grouard offers courses in life skills and labour skills; the life-skills portion of the program takes place in small discussion groups and focuses on self-image, interpersonal relationships, (family-, community-, and job-related), and on-the-job expectations. The labour-skills division offers courses in carpentry, surveying, welding, equipment maintenance, truck driving, safety, and first aid. These courses do not bring trainees up to apprenticeship levels, but they familiarize them with the types of jobs available in an industrial setting.

In 1978, 75 per cent of Grouard's curriculum was related to life skills and 25 per cent to job training, but since there was a need to increase trainees, 'employability', the two courses were given equal importance in the second year. Grouard can accommodate twenty trainees at one session; two sessions are held each year. By the summer of 1980, four groups of trainees had attended Grouard. The first group consisted of disadvantaged persons from various reserves, and although these trainees were still 'unemployable' at the end of the course, AGTL hired most of them and arranged for others to work on contract; only one remained with the company. For the second group, a different recruiting approach was used: the focus was on individuals who had good potential, but little opportunity to develop it on the reserve. Out of 150 applicants, twenty trainees were selected. Of these, fourteen graduated and were offered employment; two refused, twelve accepted. Of these seven are still working for NOVA. Students at Grouard receive financial assistance from the Unemployment Insurance Commission during their sixteen-week training course. Pending construction of the pipeline, employment outlets for Grouard graduates are NOVA, its contractors, its affiliates and subsidiaries, and other Alberta companies in the oil-and-gas industry.

The Alaska Project Division's Opportunity Measures Plan

In order to meet the terms and conditions of the Northern Pipeline Agency, the Alaska Project Division (APD) developed extensive programming that relates specifically to the construction phase of the Alberta section of the Alaska Highway Gas Pipeline Project (AHGPP). For the purposes of this study, we shall concentrate on the Opportunity Measures Plan, which is an 'equal employment' program for women and Native people seeking work in the pipeline industry. In view of the nature of this study, we shall focus on those aspects that pertain to Native people.

The Opportunity Measures Plan (OMP) was developed as a response to meet a number of objectives:

- To translate NOVA's views about Native employment into the policies of the Alaska Project Division
- To adopt the guidelines of the Northern Pipeline Agency with respect to improving the socio-economic conditions of Native people in Alberta, particularly those residing within the vicinity of the future pipeline
- To identify and try to remove artificial barriers to the employment of Native people
- To prepare trainees for employment in other industries, since pipeline construction involves only seasonal employment.

The Alaska Project Division has a staff of 150, five of whom participated in the creation of the employees' OMP. The APD Community Relations Supervisor, who is Native, and his staff drafted the OMP policies and procedures in consultation with senior officials of APD, AGTL, Foothills Pipe Line (Yukon) Ltd., Westcoast Transmission Company Ltd., the Alberta Native Secretariat, the Alberta Department of Intergovernmental Affairs, the Métis Association of Alberta, and many individual Native people.

The OMP was designed to ensure that non-Native contractors who will be building the pipeline hire as many Native people as possible, and the APD and NOVA provide Native businesses with advice, information, and bidding opportunities for contracts to be awarded during the construction of the AHGPP in Alberta. The plan also stipulates that non-Native contractors be involved in the construction process, particularly in the matter of subcontract tendering.[2] ADP and NOVA will not hire Native people directly for the construction of the pipeline, since the work will be carried out by a few major contractors, but it is their responsibility, according to the Northern Pipeline Act, to ensure that Native people in Alberta are the prime beneficiaries of employment and business opportunities arising from the AHGPP. The Alaska Project Divison, however, plays an active role in recruiting Native trainees for the AVC-Grouard Job-Readiness Training/Life-Skills Program. These trainees may eventually be hired by the major pipeline contractors; if so, they will play a watch-dog role within these companies to ensure that they conform to the directives of the OMP. An additional purpose for the Grouard courses is to prepare trainees for employment in other industries, since pipeline construction involves only seasonal employment.

The OMP as job-readiness training and life-skills program. Although the OMP is virtually identical to the program (described above) designed in 1978 for the first group of Grouard trainees, it has a few distinctions. In the past, for example, trainees received financial assistance from the Unemployment Insurance Commission (UIC); in future, if trainees do not qualify for UIC payments, they may apply for funds under the Canadian Employment and Immigration Commission's (CEIC) Adult Occupational Training program. Trainees will also have access to a counsellor, who will assist them to make the transition from a training situation to an industrial setting. The life-skills component of the program will include more specific courses: Relating to Others,

Finding a Job, Workers' Rights and Responsibilities, Money Management, and the Individual and the Community.[3] The labour-skills component will be extended to include a period of on-site familiarization with an actual work situation.

The 1978 and 1980 programs also differ in that the Alaska Project Division will be actively involved in disseminating information about Grouard training to as wide a Native audience as possible. A brochure describing AVC-Grouard's training courses has been prepared for distribution to the Native population of Alberta, especially to the ten Indian bands located in the pipeline vicinity, the closest Métis Association locals and Native Outreach offices, the Indian Associaton of Alberta, and the Métis Association of Alberta.

Dissemination of information on employment opportunities. The Native network referred to above will be kept informed of pipeline jobs as they become available. They will be informed about "the types, numbers and locations of jobs...anticipated employment dates, characteristics of pipeline employment...necessary qualifications, institutions from which training may be obtained and names and addresses of pipeline unions and project contractors."[4] These Native organizations will be encouraged to advise Foothills (Alberta) or APD of their particular needs or questions concerning the AHGPP so that the OMP can be adjusted accordingly.[5]

Methods of recruitment. Job candidates will be recruited from two sources. Names of Grouard graduates and of referrals from Native groups will be placed on two separate lists. Once candidates have been ranked according to their qualifications, both lists will be sent to pipeline contractors and unions. Candidates from the Grouard list will be given the choice of working in any area of the AHGPP in Alberta, whereas candidates from the second list will be encouraged to work in the vicinity of their homes.[6]

Union affiliation. The pipeline industry is governed by fourteen building trades and one pipeline union; unlike the NOVA employees, the AHGPP workers will be unionized.

Entrepreneurial opportunities. In order to maximize Native participation in all businesses related to construction of the pipeline, specific information will be sent to all Native groups: for example,

● A guide for bidding
● A directory of consultants who have assisted Native businesses in the past
● A description of the goods and services required for pipeline construction.

A list of Native businesses operating in Alberta will also be sent to major contractors and unions.

The basic intent of OMP's administrators in adopting this practice is that "all contracts will be awarded on the basis of competitive tenders," and that "native enterprises will compete with other native enterprises."[7] Foothills (Alberta) will also provide Native businesses with the name of an in-house specialist on contracts and the bidding process.

Implementation and monitoring. APD will advertise job openings in two Native newspapers in Alberta, *Kainai News* and *Native People*, and will request that each contractor name a staff person to interact with ADP to implement OMP, and that each contractor present "an orientation program to all their field employees, prior to their commencement of work on the project."[8] ADP will appoint a field inspector to ensure that major contractors (who may employ some four hundred to five hundred Native people) follow the directives of the Opportunities Measures Plan.[9] The Alaska Project Division has prepared two audio-visual presentations; one will be shown to supervisors and the other to employees who will be working for the major pipeline contractors. The object of these presentations is to communicate the message that Native people are a valuable resource and have the right to benefit from development projects in their communities.

Other plans. Though, at the time of these interviews, the Alaska Project Division had not received approval for the Opportunity Measures Plan from the Northern Pipeline Agency or from NOVA, it had initiated other pertinent projects:

- The compilation of a directory of educational programs and institutions offering pipeline-related training in Saskatchewan, Alberta, British Columbia, and the Yukon
- An educational award program for Native students wishing to pursue technical studies on completion of Grade 12. Three Native students per year will be sponsored for two years to the amount of $3500 per year. These students will receive a guarantee of summer employment and an offer of permanent employment on successful completion of their chosen course of study.
- APD participates in an *ad hoc* discussion group of petroleum-based companies in Alberta that are committed to increasing Native involvement in the province's economy. Other participants are Syncrude, Gulf Oil, Esso Resources, Shell Oil Ltd., Echo Bay Mines, Calgary Power, the Alberta Native Secretariat, and the federal Department of Regional and Economic Expansion.

In the process of arriving at the programs and policies described above, OMP's designers tried to determine the particular barriers that prevent Native people either from entering the labour market or from staying in it. They concluded that Native people have a different work ethic from non-Native people; that the skills Natives were taught on the reserve are seldom marketable in an industrial setting; that their family support system is different, that the jobs they do get require low-skilled, seasonal labour; that they are unfamiliar with the job-finding process; and that they are frequently the object of discrimination and stereotyping.[10] The Opportunity Measures Plan was designed to eliminate some of these barriers.

Indicators of Adaptation[11]

Employee turnover

Figures were not available to indicate how many Native people have been with AGTL since the early 1970s; respondents remarked that there are some employees in this category, but they are exceptions. Native long-term employment began to increase when the Native Employment Program was launched in 1976. In 1977 there were thirty Native people on staff; in 1978 there were forty-five, and in 1980, there were seventy-seven; this last figure represents approximately 6.4 per cent of the total number of employees working for NOVA's Gas Transmission system. Eighteen of these seventy-seven jobs are filled by Native women. One respondent remarked that Native women are often more employable than men because they have developed secretarial skills or have been involved in social work programs on their reserves.

NOVA's overall employment turnover ranges between 13 and 15 per cent, while general Native employment turnover fluctuates between 8 and 9 per cent. For the most part, employment turnover was reported to be lower in field jobs, where there is a concentration of Native people, than in the main offices.

Absenteeism

There were no data available relating to absenteeism. Nevertheless, respondents reported that Native absenteeism was a very serious problem in the first half of the 1970s, but that it had diminished remarkably since the Native Employment Program was put into place in

1976. One respondent attributed this decrease to an improvement in recruitment techniques.

Productivity
Again, no hard data were available. Respondents reported that Native productivity was certainly equal, if not superior, to that of non-Native output. These comments were made respecting quantity of work, as well as quality of performance. NOVA has put into effect a Performance and Development System whereby, every six months, each employee is expected to discuss his progress with his superior. One respondent remarked that "Once a person is trained and oriented, there is no difference in productivity but, without this training, there is a difference."

Participation
Two respondents believed that prejudice against Native employees still exists within the company, but that it is not overtly expressed. The Native recruiter is often called on to settle problems between Native workers and non-Native supervisors. Generally the misunderstandings are at this level, rather than between Native and non-Native employees. One respondent was of the opinion that interaction between Native and non-Native employees is not a problem because the Native Employment Program is based on the principle that every applicant should have similar qualifications for the same type of job.

Conclusions
NOVA's commitment to the employment of Native people manifested itself in many ways: through its support of the NORTRAN program in 1973, the AGTL Foothills Training Program and the AGTL Native Development Program in 1976, the Grouard Basic Job Readiness Training

and Life-Skills Program in 1978, and the Opportunity Measures Plan in 1980. Each of these programs, as well as outside influences, contributed to NOVA's present views about the employment of Native people. For instance, one respondent believed that government pressure in the early 1970s, as well as a recognition that corporations had a social responsibility, somehow seeped into NOVA's thinking about staff planning. More recently, the creation of the Northern Pipeline Agency in 1978 for the purpose of protecting northerners' socio-economic conditions added importance to NOVA's Native policies.

In the early days, AGTL focused on achieving a quota of Native employees that would reflect their percentage in the Alberta population; once this quota was achieved, however, a new point of view began to emerge. Where once it was believed that Native northerners should be hired because they were a local resource, and it made good business sense to employ on-site labour, NOVA now recognizes that Native people should be hired because they are competent, and because the practice supports the principle of hiring people from within the region where a company is making money. The development of human resource potential now seems to be the reason behind NOVA's Native-hiring practices. The NOVA model has many similarities with the programs we have looked at so far: it offers life skills; it recognizes the importance of educating the young; it includes women; its Native programs are planned and run by Native people; it supports and encourages Native businessmen; it consults Native organizations; it emphasizes the importance of giving special training to supervisors who will work with Native employees. But perhaps NOVA's most distinctive feature is that it recognizes officially that Native people are competent workers and therefore form a desirable resource.

It may be useful to review the conditions that have led NOVA to employ Native workers to a total of 6.5 per cent of its staff.

Equal Employment Opportunity

NOVA is committed to treating every employee equally. One respondent stated that once a Native person has been sufficiently trained and is taken on the regular work-force, he or she is treated like any other employee and has access to additional training courses, if he or she wishes. From that point on, there is no differentiation based on a person's ethnic or cultural background; the same standards apply to everyone. One Native respondent remarked that many Native employees asked not to be treated differently from non-Native employees because they want to succeed on their own merit rather than as the recipients of 'special treatment'.

Government Participation

The Government of Canada, through the Northern Pipeline Agency, influenced NOVA's Native policies, but there does not seem to be any disagreement about overall objectives between the two groups. The Canadian Employment and Immigration Commission provided $280 000 for the training of eighty Grouard trainees, and the Alberta government covered the cost of operating the Grouard facilities.

Corporate Support

NOVA has hired all the NORTRAN and Grouard trainees, though these candidates were to be taken on by pipeline contractors. NOVA has a Native co-ordinator on staff and collaborates with the Native co-ordinator of the Alaska Project Division. NOVA's president has been publicly acclaimed for his role in promoting the employment of Native people in Canada.

Vocational Schools

The Alberta Vocational Centre located in Grouard, 320 kilometres northeast of Edmonton, collaborates with NOVA and APD.

Native Participation

NOVA has hired Native recruiters since the Native Recruitment Program was launched in 1976. The person responsible for planning the Opportunity Measures Plan is of Indian ancestry. One respondent remarked that Native recruiters have a better understanding of the daily realities that a Native worker must cope with and therefore can be of greater assistance in easing the transition of Native workers to an industrial environment. He also considered Native recruiters good role models. NOVA has always consulted Native organizations in these matters.

The Selectivity Factor

With respect to the selectivity factor, NOVA's program resembles the Headstart model. Because NOVA does not want to produce failures, it is quite selective in its recruitment procedures. It tries to identify those persons who have the potential to succeed and therefore attributes considerable importance to a candidate's work experience; a steady employment background is preferred. Because NOVA does not hire known alcoholics, the risk of failure is minimized. NOVA does not stress educational requirements, but looks for candidates who have the potential for getting a job done. NOVA did not lower its entry requirements for certain jobs, but jobs were restructured in accordance with a variety of skills. The reasoning in this instance is that if Native workers have the same skills and competence as non-Native workers, there will be less cause for friction on work crews and a higher probability of mutual acceptance. To illustrate the Native perspective on this point, one Native respondent stated: "We are here to do a job, not to slide by because we are Indian. I may have got some of my jobs because I was an Indian, but you keep a job because you have good skills."

Another example of the selectivity factor is the change in recruitment criteria for Grouard candidates from one year to another. The 1978 trainees were selected from a group of disadvantaged Natives, and only one remained with NOVA; recruitment in 1979 focused on candidates who had displayed good potential, with a corresponding increase in long-term Native employment.

Proximity to Home Communities

NOVA's policies of hiring local manpower and of providing vocational training in northern Alberta indicate a recognition that programs are more effective if their clientèle does not have to leave their own communities.

Life-Skills

NOVA trainees are sent to a vocational school, and life-skills training takes place in a classroom situation, in complete isolation from the work environment.

Training Supervisors

Again, the NOVA program can be compared with the Syncrude model in that they both have developed cultural awareness seminars for managers and supervisors. As one NOVA respondent noted, although senior management has a strong commitment to Native employment, it is supervisors and managers in the middle-management category who deal directly with Native employees. For this reason, while discriminatory practices may exist, senior managers may never become aware of them. The OMP includes an audio-visual presentation for supervisors to help overcome any inequalities in the handling of employees.

Native Entrepreneurial Activities

NOVA, through the Alaska Project Division Opportunity Measures Plan, accords major importance to developing ways in which to initiate or support Native business enterprises.

A Caution

The information supplied in this section was provided by persons at the upper- and middle-management levels; two of these are of Indian ancestry. It is, therefore, difficult to draw any conclusions about the impact of NOVA's Native-recruitment program on the employees themselves. Moreover the Opportunity Measures Plan could not be evaluated, since it had not yet been implemented at the time of writing.

Notes:

1.   Northern Petroleum Industry Training Program.

2.   Alaska Project Division, *Opportunity Measures Plan - Foothills Pipe Lines (Alta.) Ltd.*, July 1980.

3.   *Ibid.*, p. 24.

4.   *Ibid.*, p. 11.

5.   *Ibid.*, p. 11.

6.   *Ibid.*, p. 12.

7.   *Ibid.*, p. 15.

8.   *Ibid.*, p. 17.

9.   *Ibid.*, p. 17.

10. *Ibid.*, p. 17.

11. The comments made in this section are applicable only to Native employment at AGTL.

6: Manitoba Telephone System

The Provincial Setting

The 1970s saw the initiation of many new social programs in Manitoba. During this period, the Government of Manitoba produced a policy statement on equal employment opportunities for women, Natives and handicapped persons. In order to combat the critical unemployment problems that northern residents —particularly Native people— were facing, the Government of Manitoba established the Northern Manpower Corps (NMC) and its Directorate in July 1971. The Northern Manpower Directorate included senior civil servants from the Manitoba government and the federal government. Its mandate was to oversee the activities of the Northern Manpower Corps, to act as consultant to NMC, and to report to the Planning and Priorities Committee of the Manitoba Cabinet. The Northern Manpower Corps was to provide various services such as recruitment, candidate selection, pre-employment counselling, industrial and urban orientation, transportation, relocation services, commuting options, on-the-job training, and family counselling. The Corps' mandate also included negotiation with companies in northern Manitoba for the provision of some of these services.

The New Careers Program of Manitoba

New Careers, originally a pilot project of the Manitoba Department of Labour and Manpower, was another of the province's new social programs. It is an on-the-job training and educational upgrading program for "people who have been unemployed, or underemployed, and are disadvantaged in terms of formal education, age, sex, ethnic background, or geographic location."[1] Though it is not stated in any of its literature, the clientèle of New Careers is mostly of Indian ancestry.

The New Careers Program is based on the premise that every human being has a right to employment, ant that adults are capable of being trained for jobs in a short period of time when these jobs are interesting, offer opportunity for growth, and are well paid. The original concept of New Careers was developed as a strategy against poverty, and it "was based on the assumption that poverty is not due to inherent personal weaknesses, but it is the result of economic, social or geographic barriers which lock a great many individuals out of mainstream-society."[2]

This program was created in November 1970 and was run by a co-ordinator assisted by a secretary. It was modelled on a federal program in the United States and operated under the jurisdiction of the Department of Education until 1978, when it was transferred to the Department of Labour and Manpower. The original goals of New Careers are still in effect, though the focus now is less on placing people in government agencies than on securing employment opportunities in the private sector. These goals are:

> To provide opportunities for interested and motivated people who have been blocked from the traditional academic routes to career development, to develop their potential....
>
> To create socially useful and meaningful jobs at the entry level, to help individuals enter the job market in areas of high need in the human services; to train people for such jobs....

To increase the efficiency and effectiveness of service through the use of paraprofessional workers; to provide a way for people who have been recipients of services to bring their experience and unique qualifications, such as specific knowledge of the language, culture and community, to the delivery of service.

To reorient government employment practices by demonstrating that the waiver of traditional recruiting patterns and credentials does not entail a lowering of standards, if accompanied by special program efforts.[3]

The implementing of these purposes involves the New Careers staff, the employer, and the trainee. New Careers staff, which includes twelve full-time and several part-time workers contacts employers, recruits, screens, and selects trainees, and provides academic upgrading. Successful candidates are offered a written contract promising employment at the end of training. Initially the contract covered a period of two years, but its length now depends on the jobs available. Trainees receive 70 per cent of the salary they would earn at entry level in their category; after six months on the job, they receive a salary increase. Additional benefits are available, such as child care, dental care, glasses, clothing, paid holidays, and sick leave. The employer provides a one- or two-year, on-the-job, training program, as well as an agreement to hire the trainee if he or she completes the program satisfactorily. The trainee spends two weeks in the class-room and six weeks on the job on a rotation basis for a period of one or two years, depending on the extent of academic upgrading required.

New Careers courses focus on techniques rather than on theory. The trainee concentrates on whatever he or she needs to know on the job; irrelevant material is eliminated. Course designers study job descriptions, break them down into specific tasks that must be accomplished, and develop appropriate material for class-room use. New careers has six

Native teachers on its staff and has developed working relationships with Native organizations in Winnipeg, with tribal and band councils from various communities, and with Canada Manpower Centres throughout Manitoba.

New Careers is funded jointly by the Government of Manitoba and two federal departments, DREE and CEIC. In accordance with a Canada/Manitoba Northlands Agreement, DREE funds 60 per cent of training courses for northern residents. Trainees in southern Manitoba receive, for one year, 80 per cent of their salary and 50 per cent of their travel and accommodation expenses from CEIC's Occupational Training Fund. The Canada Manpower Industrial Training Program covers 100 per cent of teachers' salaries.[4]

Manitoba Telephone System: Characteristics and Setting

The Manitoba Telephone System (MTS) is a Crown corporation that provides telecommunication services to the residents of the Province of Manitoba. Its headquarters are located in Winnipeg, and there are regional offices in Thompson and Brandon, as well as eighty-one district offices in Manitoba's smaller communities.

In 1970 MTS launched a Northern Service Improvement Plan that brought the telephone to thirty-seven communities (18 000 residents) in northern Manitoba; most of these people are of Indian ancestry. During the course of this eight-year project, MTS began to hire Native people primarily as interpreters to assist the linemen responsible for setting up a telephone system in each community. Eventually, however, MTS hired Native people as apprentice linemen.

In the early 1970s, MTS was experiencing difficulties in retaining district operators for its northern operations. MTS management began consultations with the Manitoba New Careers co-ordinators in September

1974, in an attempt to solve this problem, and subsequently hired its first group of New Careerists in April 1976.

Equal Employment Opportunity Program

Equal Employment Opportunity is an affirmative action program that was set up at MTS in 1975 and is still operating. In the mid-1960s, discussions were held between MTS management and representatives of the International Brotherhood of Electrical Workers (IBEW) with the object of involving more Native people in the corporation. Though no formal recruitment program was set up, representatives of MTS and IBEW reached a mutual agreement that they would try, on an informal basis, to encourage Native people to apply for jobs at MTS. This agreement had little success, chiefly because very few people of Indian ancestry had completed Grande 12, the basic educational requirement for entrance to an apprenticeship program.

A decade later, in 1976, as a result of its interest in improving the socio-economic conditions of Native people, and in response to the lead taken by the Government of Manitoba in promoting an 'equal opportunity' policy, MTS, a Crown corporation, developed its own Equal Employment Opportunity Program. The objectives of the MTS Equal Employment Opportunity Program were to increase the numbers of women, handicapped, and Native people employed by MTS in order to reflect more adequately the composition of society at large. The development of the EEO program was, in part, attributable to an affirmative action trend taking shape in the mid-1970s. More particularly, however, governments served as major catalysts in issuing directives that reinforced this trend. To some extent, MTS developed these two programs in response to changes occurring outside the organization; at the same time, the programs were developed, in part, because of individuals inside the

System who were in a position to accelerate change and who were sympathetic to the redefinition of corporate responsibility.

To achieve its objectives, MTS hired a human resources consultant in 1976 to plan and co-ordinate an Equal Employment Opportunity Program. Shortly afterwards, an EEO Committee was formed by the Chairman of the Board of MTS for the purpose of developing an EEO policy and a five-year plan of action for its implementation. Members of this committee included two MTS commissioners, two representatives of the International Brotherhood of Electrical Workers, a representative of the MTS support staff, a former director of MTS, and two *ex officio* members: the Director of Personnel and the Director of Human Resources. The last two members did not have voting privileges.

The human resources consultant, who became the MTS Director of Human Resources, investigated equal employment programs in other private corporations and studied Affirmative Action literature. Statistical analyses of MTS' occupational structure were undertaken. Among the aspects of the program analysed were, for example, the ratio of males to females and the ratio of management to non-management positions; in addition, an attempt was made to identify handicapped and Native employees. The EEO Committee drafted a policy[5] based on the collected information and a plan of action that, as its members believed, reflected MTS' organizational culture. The plan of action included processes for:

- Identifying and removing barriers to employment of Native people, women, older workers, and handicapped persons
- Designing specialized training programs
- Retraining employment interviewers and supervisors
- Assessing and rewriting company literature on careers and occupations to remove biases and stereotyping
- Publicizing the fact that MTS is an equal opportunity employer.

Objectives

The primary objective of the New Careers Program within MTS was to increase the number of Native employees in the corporation. This objective was based on the company's recognition of its social responsibility in the area it serviced. Though the System was a major employer in Manitoba, it did not, in 1976, reflect the ethnic composition of the population. Furthermore MTS had been having difficulties in communicating with its Native clientèle, which represented 80 per cent of the population it was servicing in the North. It therefore made good business sense for MTS to employ Native people who could deal with their customers in their own language. The support of New Careers thus had a pragmatic aspect that was likely to benefit the company, as well as its clients and the community.

Implementation and Functioning

The idea of instituting a New Careers program within MTS had been under discussion since 1974. In July 1975 the Manitoba Department of Education, which, at the time, was responsible for the New Careers program, proposed to the Chairman and General Manager of MTS that twelve Native northerners be encouraged to enter an apprenticeship training program in June 1976. In August 1975 the senior management of MTS accepted the proposal, and each party agreed to divide responsibility for the venture. Under the agreement, Manitoba Telephone System would provide:

- Identification of essential skills for apprenticeship entry
- On-the-job training
- A course in electricity
- Commitment to hire successful trainees
- Supervision by a journeyman.

Manitoba New Careers would provide:

- Salaries of trainees until their entry into an apprenticeship program
- Academic upgrading
- Personal services (for example, dental care, child care).

A meeting was held in September 1975 to plan the introduction of New Careers into MTS. Participants included representatives of New Careers, the Manitoba Northern Manpower Corps, the International Brotherhood of Electrical Workers, and MTS' Personnel Manager, Plant Manager, and Northern Manager. All agreed that MTS should hire New Careerists on a contract basis to work as telephone installers and repairmen in northern communities "once they had passed the apprenticeship entrance examination (grade 12 level in mathematics and physics) and had completed the electricity course successfully."[6] Once enrolled in the apprenticeship program, a New Careerist would be treated like any other employee.

Criteria of Eligibility

Individuals experiencing difficulties in social adaptation, that is, those in greatest need of assistance in entering the labour market, were the preferred candidates in the first year of New Careers. Later the criteria of eligibility changed: the second group of candidates had to be highly motivated; its members were chosen on the basis of their apparent motivation and stability. Previous work experience was not essential, but candidates had to demonstrate an interest in learning a trade and undergoing the related academic upgrading. They also had to be willing to relocate. Table 3 shows the successive steps to be undertaken by New Careerists once they are accepted into the program.

Methods of Recruitment

Between November 1975 and February 1976, the MTS/New Careers recruitment team visited eight northern communities and selected

Table 3: Career Path of New Careerists

	Activity	*Responsible Agent*
Stage I *a*	Candidate	Band councils, New Careers and MTS representatives
	Trainee orientation	MTS *b*
	Academic upgrading *c*	New Careers *d*
	On-the-job training	MTS *e*
Stage II *a*	Electricity course (AC/DC)	MTS *f*
	Apprentice entrance exam	MTS
	Further on-the-job training to level 7 of the IBEW collective agreement	MTS *g*
Stage III *h*	Permanent employment with MTS as an apprentice	In northern communities

Notes

a. Stages I and II may take one year, subject to the trainee's qualifications on entry and aptitude.
b. At Thompson, Manitoba.
c. Grade 12 in mathematics and physics.
d. At Thompson in 1976; at Winnipeg in 1977.
e. At Thompson and in surrounding communities.
f. At Winnipeg Training Centre.
g. In northern communities.
h. This is a four-year stage for all MTS apprentices, where their technical training is advanced in combination with field training.

twenty-four candidates. These men were flown to Thompson in March 1976 to be interviewed by a selection committee consisting of a New Careers representative, the MTS Northern Manager and Plant Manager, and a Native journeyman. After three days of interviews, the committee chose seven trainees and seven alternates; the successful candidates were asked to report to work on 5 April 1976. During a two-day orientation session, on 5 and 6 April, trainees were informed of the schedule they would be expected to follow for the next year and told that every two months, their foreman would be filling out, on their behalf, a report entitled 'Analysis of Development and Training Requirements'. These forms would be sent to the Plant Manger in Thompson and to the New Careers representative in Winnipeg. Trainees were also told that the Native lineman who had interviewed them in March would visit each one of them every two months to see whether they were experiencing any problems relating to their new situations. The lineman would be expected to report his findings in writing to the Northern Manager and to the New Careers representative.

In 1977 the MTS/New Careers recruitment team visited twelve communities and selected twenty-four candidates, who were then flown into Thompson for a final interview. Seven candidates were asked to report to work in Thompson on 9 May 1977.

Following a period of consultation and evaluation of the New Careers Program, the Manager of MTS' Northern Operations recommended to the MTS Executive Committee that the program be implemented for a third year, but that a life-skills component be added to help trainees adapt to an industrial milieu. The Executive Committee was prepared to support this recommendation, but the Government of Manitoba imposed temporary cutbacks on some of its programs; one of these was New Careers. The Manitoba New Careers program was reinstated in 1979.

Indicators of Adaptation

Employee turnover

The status of the first group of New Careerists, who were hired in March 1976, is as follows:

- Four trainees completed the New Careers Training Program, passed the apprentice entrance examination, and became regular MTS employees. Later, three of them were terminated, after an average stay of eighteen months, because of frequent absenteeism; the fourth is still working for MTS.

- One trainee resigned after six months as a New Careerist because he had found a better-paying job.

- Two trainees were terminated before completing their training because of absenteeism.

The second group, hired in April 1977, was made up of six trainees, including one replacement. Their status is as follows:

- Three were terminated early in the program because of absenteeism.

- One was terminated after six months because he was unable to cope with the academic upgrading requirement.

- Three completed the training program, passed the entrance examination, and became regular MTS apprentices in January 1978. They are still with the System.

There is a significant difference in the academic performance of the two groups, which may be explained, in part, by the change in eligibility criteria from one year to the next. The three trainees who passed the apprenticeship entrance examination in 1976 obtained an average mark of 60 per cent; the three candidates who were successful in 1977 obtained an average of 82 per cent. Of the four trainees who completed the New Careers Program, two have become linemen, and two are apprentices. All four are still working for MTS.

Absenteeism

Absenteeism was the major cause for termination of New Careerists in 1976 and 1978, in spite of leniency shown to them by their supervisors.

Productivity

In interviews with eleven respondents who had been in a position to observe the behaviour of MTS crews, we learned that there appears to be no difference between the productivity of Natives and non-Natives. Team productivity would, of course, suffer from frequent absenteeism. One veteran foreman was of the opinion that Native productivity was initially higher than that of non-Natives, but that eventually it adjusted to the norm.

Participation

New Careerists were members of the International Brotherhood of Electrical Workers, but were not active participants, since their work was usually performed in remote areas. They were in contact with the Manager of the Northern Operation on a regular basis, particularly when they were taking courses in Thompson. The manager monitored their progress in collaboration with the Manitoba New Careers representative and the Equal Employment Opportunity co-ordinator. Trainees had access to a shop steward, who also assisted them in solving problems as these arose; he believed that daily interaction between Native and non-Native workers in a work setting did much to reduce one group's apprehensions and misunderstandings about the other.

In one discussion with a Native trainee and a Native co-ordinator, we learned that New Careerists interacted socially with other employees to a greater extent when they were working in remote communities than when they worked in urban communities. When they were posted in Thompson, their social interaction was limited to sporting events. One non-Native foreman agreed with these observations; he considered that it was more difficult for friendships to form between Natives and non-Natives in an urban setting because differences in life-style, peer pressure, and family obligations are more constraining in larger communities.

Job satisfaction

A Native New Careerist and a Native lineman who acted as co-ordinator to the program reported that New Careers was one of the best programs they had encountered on their reserves, and they expressed the hope that it would be reinstated. They also considered the MTS Equal Employment Opportunity Program a positive measure to alleviate the unemployment of Native people. They were both satisfied with their personal situation because they earned good wages, had the opportunity to learn a 'portable' trade, and were able to work outdoors in the vicinity of their community.

Respondents' Observations

Since the respondents had had two years to reflect on the New Careers experience, many of them had suggestions about how a reinstated program could be improved. Some recommendations called for:

- Life-skills training. A life-skills course, where the distinctions between Native and non-Native value systems are clarified, should precede academic upgrading and on-the-job training.
- Native participation. Native people should be involved in the planning phase of the next New Careers program. Former graduates could act as resource persons.
- Non-Native participation. "There should be ample time built into such a program to develop the support, understanding, and commitment that is required of supervisory and managerial staff, and of fellow employees."

Conclusions

There are many ways in which the New Careers Program at the Manitoba Telephone System was innovative. Some of the important characteristics and innovations of the program are noted below.

Acceptance of New Careerists

The MTS policy is that New Careerists should be treated like any other employee once they have reached the apprenticeship stage. From the day of their entrance into the program, trainees are given time to adjust to their work environment, to the academic upgrading process, and to the reality of working for a large corporation.

Management Support

The General Manager of MTS was supportive of New Careers. Even more important, the fact that the Premier of Manitoba initiated a Northern Manpower Directorate to look into ways of creating employment opportunities for Native northerners had a very positive impact on this program.

Educational Support

In programs described in earlier chapters, academic upgrading took place in vocational schools or community colleges. In the MTS program, academic upgrading was given at the Manitoba New Careers Centre in Winnipeg. Technical courses were given either at the Thompson office of MTS or at its Winnipeg Training Centre. The upgrading was handled more or less 'in house' and was geared to the strict requirements of a particular job.

Native Involvement

A Native journeyman was involved in the New Careers program from the start, not only to provide training in the line trade, but also to serve as a link between Native trainees and non-Native trainees, co-workers and supervisors.

Proximity to Home Communities

The New Careers Program gave Native trainees an opportunity to work on or near their reserves. Most respondents reported that the trainees preferred this arrangement.

Group Dynamics

MTS organized training workshops for supervisors. Program staff believed these sessions had served to reduce potential conflict between supervisors and Native workers.

The Selectivity Factor

The MTS assessment of the success of its program was based on the number of successful graduates. In its first year, MTS focused on hiring those who were in greatest need of assistance in entering the labour market, that is, those who had severe social problems. Since the first year's results were poor, entrance requirements for the second group of applicants were tightened: attention was given to those candidates who seemed motivated to work and who did not demonstrate any 'social problem'.

Notes

1.   Ellen Gordon, "The New Careers Program of Manitoba, 1979". A paper presented by Ellen Gordon and Peter Dubienski to a National Conference sponsored by The Social Planning Council of Winnipeg and the Canadian Council on Social Development, Winnipeg, Manitoba, 21-23 October 1979, p. 4.

2.   *Ibid.*, p. 1.

3.   *Ibid.*, p. 3

4.   *Ibid.*, p. 13.

5.   See Appendix.

6.   Manitoba Telephone System, Memorandum re New Careers, September 1975.

7: INCO Metals Company, Manitoba Division

Characteristics and Setting

INCO Metals Company is the major operating arm of INCO Limited, a Canada-based multinational corporation engaged in the production of primary metals, formed metal products, batteries, and related electrical and electronic products. This company is the largest producer of nickel in the world. It has production operations in Sudbury, Thompson, Jakarta and Guatemala City, and marketing offices in New York, London, Toronto and Melbourne. Its head office is located in Toronto. INCO employs 53 000 people in twenty-seven countries and spans four continents. Sixty-two per cent of its shareholders are Canadian residents.

We are concerned here with the Manitoba Division of INCO Metals Company, which is located in Thompson. It comprises a mine, a smelter, a refinery and a research laboratory, and employs 2600 people. Company officials estimate that approximately 250 people of Indian ancestry work in INCO's Manitoba Division.

The Northern Employment Program

History

INCO has been hiring Native people since it opened its doors in 1960. However, the first thrust to increase the number of Native employees was made in 1965, when the problem of high employee turnover was most acute. Till then recruitment had been taking place in all parts of Canada and, consequently, the majority of the work-force was from outside Manitoba. Workers and their families often found it difficult to adjust to life in a northern environment and would return to their points of origin after a brief stay with the company. INCO management studied the problem of staff turnover and concluded that the core of a stable work-force would be found in the immediate environment of its Thompson enterprise. If the company focused its recruitment activities on candidates who were comfortable living in northern Manitoba, it would be more successful in retaining employees on a long-term basis. Northern Manitobans, the largest number of whom are of Native extraction, were seen as the most suitable source of manpower. Another factor that reinforced the company's decision to adjust its hiring policy was a request by the federal Department of Indian Affairs that INCO increase the number of Indians in its work-force. From 1965 to 1968, INCO's Director of Personnel worked in collaboration with representatives of Indian Affairs to place their referrals. During that period, Native organizations did not exercise any pressure on INCO to hire more Native people, probably because they were embroiled in jurisdictional disputes of their own with the federal and provincial governments.

In the late 1960s, INCO organized underground and surface tours of its plant facilities for Native chiefs and band councils. The company hoped that once the chiefs returned to their reserves, they would persuade some of their people to apply to INCO for permanent employment. In 1969 INCO hired a Native recruiter, who began to visit Native communities and reserves in order to attract more recruits. He worked in collaboration with the Manitoba Métis Federation, which assisted in relocating new INCO employees in Thompson. Recruitment efforts were not too successful in this period, apparently for three reasons:

●   INCO did not have a formal Native-recruitment program.

●   There were not enough counsellors available to provide life-skills training.

●   Manitoba Hydro launched a major project in northern Manitoba, which opened up many new jobs.

The Manitoba Métis Federation began referring Native people to Manitoba Hydro because the Federation was funded by the Manitoba government and felt obliged to give priority to the province's major project. INCO could not compete for Native northerners at that time because the Manitoba Hydro jobs, though short term, were more appealing to Natives, since they involved working outdoors rather than in a plant or in a mine.

By this time, that is, 1971/1972, Indian Affairs was less visible in Thompson than it had been, and two other government agencies became very active. The Canada Manpower Centre began to relocate people in Thompson for INCO and other firms, and the Manitoba Northern Manpower Corps provided employment-counselling services to Native people, as well as assistance in obtaining living accommodation. Good working relationships were beginning to develop among the Canada Manpower Centre, the Northern Manpower Corps, and the Manitoba Métis Federation. Nevertheless, these agencies could not keep up with INCO's manpower needs. At this point INCO management decided to structure the company's own Native-recruitment program. The program was created in 1972 and was called the 'Northern Employment Program'. In 1975 the Employee Relations Branch was formed to take responsibility for the Northern Employment Program and for relations between employees and supervisors.

In the late 1970s the University of Brandon hosted a seminar for INCO supervisors, for the purpose of discussing the special requirements of training Native employees. As part of this program, supervisors had to live for three weeks in Native communities to become familiar with the Native way of life. These seminars were later discontinued.

Objectives

The official objective of the Northern Employment Program is "to utilize the source of manpower located close to the company's operation in northern Manitoba by recruiting, employing, training, and retraining northern residents of Manitoba in its Thompson operation" in order "to improve the stability of the Native employees within the work force and increase the proportion of these employees in all phases of its operation."[1]   The purpose of the Northern Employment Program is to address "the company's priority in meeting the needs of its manpower requirements in its operation in northern Manitoba."[2] INCO's policy goes one step further in stating that "should an economic situation occur which requires the reduction in production and manpower levels of the Company, the Company's commitment does not inhibit its present or future obligation in its employment objective in the area of Northern employment. Senior management has expressed an ongoing commitment to continue its efforts in the Northern Employment Program."[3]

Originally the goal of the Northern Employment Program was to increase the number of Native people on staff, but it is now centred on finding ways to retain Native employees.   The Northern Employment Program does not offer a variety of Native programs, but it assists people to obtain help for themselves by directing them to the appropriate resource person when a problem arises.   This policy is based on the principle that self-help leads to self-development.

Implementation and Functioning

The Northern Employment Program was initiated in 1972 by a director and a Native co-ordinator, who report to the Superintendent of Employee Relations; the Superintendent reports directly to the President of the Manitoba Division. The program's main activities consisted in:

- Hiring Native employees
- Visiting Native communities
- Placing the right candidate in the right job
- Monitoring the progress of Native employees
- Liaising with governmental, social and Native agencies in Thompson.

These activities evolved over the years, and INCO now interacts informally with a different group of government agencies. When the first Native co-ordinator resigned in 1977, he was replaced by another Native person. The position of co-ordinator has been expanded to include participation in the Manitoba Native Employment Committee, which includes representatives from the federal and provincial governments, the private sector, labour unions and Native organizations. The Committee meets every six weeks to discuss ways of creating employment opportunities, training programs, life-skills programs, and other pertinent matters. It is an offshoot of the Interprovincial Association of Native Employment, of which the INCO Native co-ordinator is also a member.

It has always been company policy to hire a Native person who can speak Cree as co-ordinator of the Native Employment Program. The co-ordinator is also expected to have experience in employment or personnel matters and in working with Native communities. Not many Native employees were hired during 1977 and 1978 because of cut-backs in government spending, and also because of the difficulties that began to affect the nickel market. This failure to hire Natives contravened the stated company policy mentioned above, that is, INCO's promise that economic conditions would not deter the company from its goal of hiring more Native employees. INCO nevertheless kept in touch with the various northern communities and Native organizations in Manitoba and, in the summer of 1979, when the economic situation permitted, hired 122 people of Indian ancestry.

Since 1979 the Native co-ordinator has been accompanied in his recruitment visits to Native communities and Indian reserves by a Native-relocation officer of the Manitoba Department of Labour and Manpower and by a co-ordinator from Native Outreach. These people provide potential recruits with information about the nature of jobs available at INCO, on-the-job training and counselling programs, housing and schooling facilities, other services available in Thompson, and the process of relocating.

Criteria of eligibility

The preferred candidate for INCO's Northern Employment Program demonstrates, during a preliminary interview, that he is self-motivated, adaptable, and willing to relocate. Preference is given to applicants who have an industrial background and at least two years' working experience. INCO's policy is preferential hiring of people within the communities of northern Manitoba; when all suitable applicants from this area have been hired, the company recruits in southern Manitoba. Only when these two sources have been fully explored, does INCO recruit outside the province in all parts of Canada. INCO makes its support services available to all employees, regardless of their ethnic or cultural background, and directs those with special needs to the appropriate governmental or social agency in order to facilitate their integration into the company.

Methods of recruitment

There are three sources of Native recruitment at INCO, of which the first is the most successful.

- Visits to Native communities by INCO representatives
- 'Walk-ins' at the Native employment office in Thompson
- Referrals from Canada Manpower Centres, Native Outreach and the Manitoba Métis Federation.

Relocation services

The Relocation Service of the Manitoba Department of Labour and Manpower was set up in 1979. This step was taken at the suggestion of an INCO representative, who thought that it would be more efficient for one agency only to deal with the relocation of INCO employees. Previously relocations had been handled by the Manitoba Northern Manpower Corps and the Manitoba Métis Federation.

The Department of Manpower and Labour hired a co-ordinator and a home adviser who work as a team. The co-ordinator travels on behalf of INCO to Native communities to inform them about the Relocation Program. He interviews families who are candidates for the Program, deals with rental agents, and provides counselling to families who have migrated to Thompson. Counselling is also provided to the candidate who comes to Thompson for a few days to find out if he could adapt to its environment; at the end of this period, the candidate returns to his community, where he will make a final decision. The relocation officer also offers INCO representatives an opinion on the likelihood of the candidate's remaining in Thompson.

The home adviser, when informed of the pending arrival of a new employee, enquires if relocation services are needed; if so, she assists in finding suitable accommodation, processes the lease, and pays the first month's rent, which can range from $225 to $275 per month for a home with one or two bedrooms. (This housing is subsidized by INCO.) Families must have at least one child to qualify for relocation. Once the family has moved in, the home adviser arranges to visit twice a week at first. She visits less often as the family becomes independent. She focuses on teaching the housewife to cook, use and maintain appliances, budget, and make use of day-care services, schools, social services, and recreational facilities. Courses in these areas are given in the daytime, but the husband usually does not participate, since he may be at work or asleep if he works the night-shift. The home adviser also organizes a seminar once a month, which husbands and wives usually attend together.

These counsellors stated that the main difficulties that relocated families experience are loneliness, boredom, pressures resulting from visits from an extended family, the high cost of living in Thompson, fear or the part of those who work underground, alienation from non-Native society, and discrimination. Some problems are job related: for example, some Native employees would rather quit than confront their bosses. Counsellors try to settle misunderstandings when they have been made aware of them by talking to the shift boss involved.

Another serious problem that these counsellors have observed is the difficulties that relocated families experience with respect to the school system. There is only one Native teacher in Thompson; nothing in the curriculum deals with Native culture; Native children do not know whether they can trust their teachers or their schoolmates, and parents have difficulty in relating to teachers. These two respondents saw the need for Native co-ordinators who could provide liaison between the school and the home in order to ease some of these tensions. One Native respondent remarked that Native migrants to the city suffer from discrimination. "Discrimination is evenly spread throughout the population," he claimed; "it's a fact of life that we have to deal with every second day."

Indicators of Adaptation

Employee turnover

Before the Northern Employment Program was initiated in 1972, the overall turnover of personnel was a staggering 100 to 150 per cent per year. The recruitment and training costs that this kind of turnover entailed were also staggering, as were the losses in productivity and the impact on employee morale.   Since the company began to practice preferential hiring of local people, overall employee turnover has diminished; it now stands at about 35 per cent. In 1979 the average length of stay for people hired in northern Manitoba was eight months, whereas for people hired from southern Manitoba it was 2.8 months. Though these figures represent high employee turnover, they do support the theory that it is more efficient to hire local people.

As far as Native employees are concerned, the only figures available were for the last three quarters of 1979 and the first quarter of 1980. Native-employee turnover was no better and no worse than non-Native-employee turnover in the last three quarters of 1979. However, Native turnover increased to 60 per cent in the first quarter of 1980 for no apparent reason; this percentage applies only to those who were hired in 1979. Forty per cent of Native workers who quit in the first quarter of 1980 left without giving notice or an explanation. An investigation was under way at the time of these interviews to determine why this situation occurred. Many Native people worked for INCO for an average of a year and then quit. These same individuals would return at a later date and, if their employment record was reasonable, they would be rehired. One manager observed that Native workers sometimes quit *en masse* , and he thought the chief reason was that they were homesick. According to the collective agreement that governs INCO employees (the Manitoba Mines Act), an employee is automatically terminated after ten days' absence without notice. Under these conditions, an employee is considered to have voluntarily resigned and is consequently removed from the payroll.

Absenteeism

Absenteeism fluctuates between 10 and 15 per cent, but it is no more significant among Native workers than among non-Native workers.

Productivity

Since most jobs are performed by crews or teams, it is difficult to determine an individual's productivity. It is possible to know the output of a particular shift or crew, but no breakdown of those figures was available. Issues of productivity are resolved between crew members themselves and the shift boss. One respondent stated that the Division's overall productivity had increased over the years, partly because of major improvements in technology, and partly because the work-force is better trained. Safety measures are very important in a mining operation, and INCO put into place in the early 1970s a shared responsibility system which requires that each person in the organization be involved in the safety of his co-workers. One non-Native respondent expressed the conviction that overall productivity would increase if INCO hired more Native employees.

Participation

Since they work on crews, miners spend most of their time with the same four or five people. Crews include Native and non-Native workers, though at one time INCO developed Native crews who worked under the supervision of Native supervisors. According to two managers, this system was not satisfactory for two reasons:

- Native people considered they were being ostracized because they were labelled as 'different'.
- Some Native supervisors had higher expectations of Native employees than of non-Natives.

This situation led to conflicts or, more frequently, to 'quitting'. Crews have luncheon meetings in the mine, where they discuss safety regulations, employee relations, productivity, and health standards. Job demonstrations are also given on these occasions. Native employees attend these meetings as often as other workers, but they do not participate to the same extent.   Similarly, Native workers participate very little in union meetings.

Native workers might not initially be as comfortable with their supervisors as non-Native workers, but this also depends on the style and personality of the supervisor.   If a Native employee has a work-related problem, he may quit or he may consult the Native co-ordinator, but he rarely discusses the problem with his shift boss.   If a Native employee thinks that he has been discriminated against, he has access to an Employment Relations representative or to the Employee Relations Board.   Two respondents in management positions reported that Native workers had never resorted to these referees.

INCO sponsors hockey teams and baseball teams.   There are refinery teams and underground teams, and Natives and non-Natives are members of the same teams.   The hockey stars, however, are mostly Native.   INCO organizes a Christmas party and tours of the plants for the families of workers.   The company supports many agencies in Thompson: the YMCA, the Multicultural Centre, the Manitoba Métis Federation, the Manitoba Indian Brotherhood (MIB), to name a few.   Opportunities for social interaction between Natives and non-Natives are available in Thompson, but many psychological barriers prevent people from taking advantage of them.

Respondents' Obervations

Respondents considered the Northern Employment Program effective, but offered a few suggestions for improving it.   These suggestions are summarized below.

Life Skills

INCO should run its own life-skills program that would allow Native trainees and their families to move into a small centre where they could become familiar with urban and industrial life before entering a real working environment.

Supervisors' Training

A special seminar for supervisors has been offered at the University of Brandon to acquaint these people with Native culture. This practice should be revived.

Follow-up

The Northern Employment Program should expand its follow-up function. More effort should be put into finding out why Native-employee turnover is so high. The development of a Native program should include an analysis of the nature of the available labour force in Northern Manitoba.

Conclusions

INCO's Northern Employment Program is strictly a recruitment program aimed at hiring as many Native northerners as possible in order to keep personnel-turnover costs at a minimum. INCO does not state officially, as did MTS, that it hires Native people because they are competent workers, but seems to make the assumption that Native people are good workers. The fact that INCO does not offer any built-in special programs for Native employees can also be interpreted as an indication that Native people are not considered different from non-Natives. INCO interacts with the Department of Manpower and Labour, which offers life-skills counselling to Native families who have migrated to Thompson, but the Native worker has access to the same training programs as non-Native employees once he has been hired.

It is perhaps only in the pre-employment phase of employee-employer relationships that INCO treats Native people differently from non-Natives: special efforts are made to recruit Native people in their home communities, and a Native co-ordinator, a Native relocation officer, and a Native Outreach representative work together to contact potential Native workers and to explain to them what moving to Thompson would entail.

Chief Characteristics of the Northern Employment Program

Equality
The Northern Employment Program is based on a policy that every employee must be treated equally. Once a Native person is hired by INCO, he receives no preferential treatment.

Government participation
There is no direct government funding of Native programs at INCO, since the only Native program in existence is a recruitment program. However, the Government of Manitoba participates indirectly by funding the relocation services for INCO employees through its Department of Manpower and Labour. INCO also received Canada Manpower Industrial Training Program (CMITP) funds, but these were not earmarked specifically for Native employees. They were available to all employees involved in a training program.

Corporate support
INCO pays the salaries of two senior managers who work almost exclusively at putting into practice the objectives of the Northern Employment Program. Many other employees give time to this program on an occasional basis.

Educational support
Keewatin Community College in Thompson offers apprenticeship training programs to INCO employees, whether Native or non-Native, after they

have been on staff for a year. The Government of Manitoba also sponsors a four-year apprenticeship program in the mining trade, to which Native people have access.

Native involvement
It has been company policy since 1969 to have on staff a Native recruiter.

Group dynamics
Crews are mixed at INCO, and Native and non-Native workers were reported to interact without conflict. INCO employs individuals from a variety of ethnic and racial groups and, consequently, Native workers are simply part of a mixed environment.

Eligibility for employment
INCO's criteria for hiring employees resemble those of other companies in that they stress the importance of a candidate's motivation, but they are more demanding in that they require an industrial background and two years' experience. Respondents admitted that these two conditions were hard to meet in northern Manitoba, and that they occasionally were flexible about them.

Life skills
INCO trainees receive life-skills training from a Government of Manitoba family counsellor.

Notes

1. INCO Metals Company policy statement on its Northern Employment Program.

2.   *Ibid.*

3.   *Ibid.*

8: Conclusions

It is hoped that this study, through describing Native-employment programs in six firms, has met its principal objective: to demonstrate the types of organizational arrangements that are conducive to the realization of a successful Native-employment program. Though the firms differ in size, in points of view, and in management style, they share the conviction that Native people make up an important and valuable element of Canada's human resource potential, and that they must no longer be overlooked in any overall manpower-planning program.

As we have seen in preceding chapters, there are many common elements among the six case-studies, including the firms' reasons for creating their own programs, their objectives, and their methods of implementation. However, the most obvious common element is that these firms have openly committed themselves to alleviating the problems of urban Native employment. We shall now consider what can be learned from their experiences.

Obviously, the design of a Native-employment program will always be influenced by the various factors that define a firm's internal and external environment. A firm's internal environment is determined by its financial resources, its size, its management style, its products, its goal. A firm's external environment is determined by its clientèle, the characteristics of the region in which it operates, market conditions, government legislation, the economy, and the human resources among whom it recruits its employees. Since these factors vary from one firm to another, and since firms have little or no control over their external environment, it is only within their internal environment that they are in a position to plan and execute innovation. Therefore there is no one formula or model that can be applied unilaterally under any given circumstances. To be effective, a Native-employment program must be created to meet a particular set of circumstances and must take into account the organization and functional methods of a particular firm.

In spite of the need for programs that are 'tailor made' to meet particular circumstances, significant factors of a general nature emerge from these case-studies that could explain the success or survival of some programs. A firm attempting to design the ideal program, should give attention to the following points, which include both suggestions made by respondents during the interview process and conclusions reached by the researcher.

At the design stage of a Native-employment program, companies might consider some of the following steps:

1. Identify barriers to Native employment and develop plans to eliminate those within their control

2. Examine Native-employment programs that have been set up in other firms

3. Re-examine their occupational structure and determine how it can best match the skills of Native applicants to the jobs available, or how some job descriptions can be rewritten to accommodate more Native people. Firms should be able to recognize human resource potential and modify their needs accordingly.

4. Acquire knowledge of the cultural and historical backgrounds of the various Native groups residing in the communities from which they intend to recruit

5. Define the objectives and/or goals of the Native program(s). This might be achieved through framing and answering certain specific questions relating to the organization and operation of a given firm. For example: Why is the Native-employment program being created? What is it intended to achieve? Who will benefit?

6. State clearly its Native-employment policy and take the necessary steps to ensure that all employees are aware of that policy and do not perceive it as a welfare activity

7. Disseminate information about its Native programs to as many Native groups as possible. To be effective, a Native program must be visible. Claims of an 'open-door' policy towards Native recruits are meaningless if no one ever sees a Native person working for the claimant. Moreover, if a company does not advertise its Native-recruitment program, Native people will assume that that company does not hire Natives, and they will not be encouraged to apply.

8. Sensitize upper and middle management to the particular conditions that Native employees must face in a non-Native environment. These may include overt prejudice, subtle discrimination, indifference, hostility, paternalism and patronizing. Middle management is often guilty of these practices and, to change the situation, upper management has a responsibility to make its commitment to Native programs known and accepted throughout the system.

9. Consult as extensively as possible, at the program-design stage, with Native organizations and Native people on the employment and training needs of Natives

10. Involve Native employees in the implementation and management of Native programs, but ensure that they are experienced in working with Native people and are competent in these jobs. Most

respondents believe that Native recruiters and co-ordinators are more effective than non-Native recruiters because they usually speak a Native language, are familiar with the Native recruits' home environment and with the implications of moving from a reserve or a small community to an urban centre, and, more important, because they provide positive role models.

11. At an early stage of planning, contact vocational schools or community colleges that might assist companies in providing Native employees with academic upgrading and/or specialized training. These institutions are also good sources of recruitment and usually offer career-orientation sessions where Native students can learn about employment opportunities.

12. Open lines of communication with government departments and agencies whose clientèle is of Indian ancestry so that Native people can benefit from mechanisms that are already in place: referrals, consultation, training courses, special funding, orientation, life skills, relocation services, and so on

13. Sponsor special training courses for managers and supervisors who will have direct responsibility for Native employees

14. Develop cultural awareness seminars for Native and non-Native employees so that they can acquire a better understanding of one another's culture and value systems, enjoy a better working climate, and appreciate that both groups have a responsibility for changing attitudes

15. Involve union representatives of unionized firms in the planning phase of Native programs in order to prevent the introduction of additional pressures or constraints once these programs have been implemented. Discussions should deal with the issue of 'special status' for Native employees. For example: Should Native employees receive special consideration in the first place? If so, for

how long can or should this status be maintained? How should the policies adopted be communicated to the membership?

16. Allow Native employees time to adjust to their new work environment and not immediately place on them the same expectation of performance as on those who do not bear the additional burden of having to surmount social and cultural barriers. Some respondents remarked that if Native people stay with a company for the time required for their training, they usually become long-term employees. Problems of adjustment are more prevalent during the training period of Native employees, and they often quit in discouragement rather than confront their employers with any difficulty they may be experiencing. Companies therefore should show some flexiblity toward Native employees for the two or three years it takes to learn a trade and to adjust to the demands of an industrial milieu.

17. Develop training programs in all aspects of company operations so that Native employees have access to a variety of occupations at all levels of the organization

18. Build a career-counselling element into Native programs and monitor the progress of Native employees so that they do not become locked into dead-end occupations

19. Consult with Native leaders or organizations before embarking on a life-skills program. Too often life-skills courses imply that the Euro-Canadian's life-style is superior to the Native person's, and that it is up to the Native person alone to change his or her ways. Respondents were divided on the usefulness of providing a mock industrial milieu where a Native trainee and his or her family could spend six to eight weeks in order to receive life-skills training before moving to a real urban/industrial setting. The Oo-Za-We-Kwun centre in Northern Manitoba is an example of such a milieu:

it provided Native people with both life-skills training and training in the trades or in elementary management skills.

20. Recognize that the provision of a variety of programs and services might be necessary to accommodate the different categories of Native employees, and that such a package could be developed incrementally as needs are identified. These needs could be served by the provision of social, cultural, recreational, educational and incentive programs, among others.

21. Ensure that local Native entrepreneurs benefit from the presence of any companies located in a given community. Such companies could, for example, provide a market for Native businesses, offer support services such as consultation, management counselling, market analyses, and financial information.

22. Assess local human resource potential and hire, insofar as possible, residents of the area of its activities; send recruiters to remote Native communities

23. Ensure that the ratio of staff to trainees in any Native-employment program is adequate to permit proper training and sustain morale and productivity of workers

24. Analyse the reasons for high Native-employee turnover, when it occurs, and recognize that some management practices may have to be modified in order to lower high turnover. It is not satisfactory to make assumptions about the reasons why Native employees leave their jobs. The reason may often be a matter of poor communications, and simple solutions may be found. Though most respondents indicated that high Native-employee turnover was the most serious problem they had encountered, some were of the opinion that Native-employee turnover is lower than non-Native turnover in Northern communities.

25. Evaluate Native productivity and consider that, as most

respondents pointed out, it is usually higher than non-Native productivity; design the Native-employment program with this most positive aspect of Native employment in mind

26. Consider the implications of uprooting Native employees and their families: Does the firm offer services that help the Native family to overcome the shock of leaving its home community and the stress that accompanies the resulting feelings of isolation? Managers should ask themselves if they honestly believe that they have a responsibility towards the people they displace. If a company assumes that its objective is long-term employment of Native workers, it might ponder whether, strictly from an economic perspective, it can afford *not* to provide the infrastructure that increases the likelihood of a transplanted Native family's successful adaptation to an urban environment. Respondents mentioned that those companies that offer Native persons employment in the vincinity of their home communities are usually more successful than others in retaining a stable work-force. Family ties are particularly important to Native people and often have a direct bearing on their approach to job mobility. As this study has shown, some workers choose to commute 180 kilometres a day in order to continue living in their home communities.

In summary, there is no perfect formula for the creation of Native-employment programs, but there is a very large number of factors to consider. The author hopes that the conclusions stated above will prepare the ground for those companies that are beginning to think about Native people as a valuable human resource. The field of Native-employment programs is relatively uncultivated, but it is not barren. Serious efforts are being made, trends are emerging, attitudes are changing, and Native people must be kept informed of these developments, but, more important, they must be full participants in the process of defining their place in the urban work-force.

Appendix

Equal Employment Opportunity Policy[1]

Equal opportunity for all employees is policy in the Manitoba Telephone System. This means that all employees, regardless of race, nationality, religion, colour, sex, age, marital or family status, ethnic or national origin, or political beliefs shall be afforded equal access to career paths and training and development which reflect their personal choice, interest and ability. All occupations in MTS must be open to anyone who has the qualifications to carry out the duties/functions inherent in them; otherwise, both the employee and the System will not reap the full advantages of competence, energy and innovation that exist within all MTS employees.

Maximized System growth and progress will only be achieved if we enable employees to utilize their potential to the fullest extent possible. This means that all of us must begin to think about our career goals and to rethink our traditional attitudes toward job roles. In the past, we have tended to consider management jobs and craft jobs as exclusively open to men while Traffic Operator, Clerical and Secretarial jobs have been the preserve of women. Job opportunities for persons of native origin have been few despite the fact that they represent a significant proportion of the population of the North. The physically and mentally handicapped and the older worker are continually faced with problems in the job market which are often the result of incorrect assumptions about their capabilities. Efforts must be made to ensure that men and women from all backgrounds have the opportunity to progress in Management or Plant, Marketing or Commercial, Personnel or Traffic, Engineering or Planning, or anywhere else according to the principles of merit and free choice.

To achieve the full impact of this policy, Affirmative Action is necessary. Affirmative Action recognizes that certain groups are not represented equitably within MTS and it is therefore a program designed to accelerate equalized opportunity of employment and progression in MTS for all present and potential employees in all occupations, in accordance with job requirements. It further recognizes a commitment on the part of both the System and the employee to utilize available resources to the fullest possible extent, in order to ensure the fulfillment of career objectives.

Affirmative Action will result in: inventories of skill being conducted; personal assessment opportunity and career counselling being offered along with varied approaches to development and training which recognizes continuing education and training as part of the total career process.

This approach to total human resource development in MTS will require the support and commitment of all employees and managers, but it will result in greater satisfaction of all employees and maximized growth for the System.

Note

1. Source: Manitoba Telephone System, Personnel Department
    (Winnipeg).

Bibliography

Breton, Raymond and Grant, Gail, eds. *Analysis of Government Programs and Policies Relating to Urban Natives.* Montreal: The Institute for Research on Public Policy, 1983.

Breton, Raymond and Grant, Gail. *Urban Institutions and People of Indian Ancestry.* Occasional Paper No. 5. Montreal: The Institute for Research on Public Policy, 1978.

Brody, Hugh. *Indians on Skid Row.* Ottawa: Information Canada. 1971.

Cumming, Peter A. and Mickenberg, Neil H., eds. *Native Rights in Canada.* Toronto: The Indian-Eskimo Association of Canada in association with General Publishing Co. Limited, 1971.

Deines, Anne; Littlejohn, Catherine; Hunt, Terence. *Native Employment Patterns in Alberta's Athabasca Oil Sands Region.* Prepared for the Alberta Oil Sands Environmental Research Program by the Canadian Institute for Research in the Behavioural and Social Sciences, 1979.

Dosman, Edgar J. *Indians: The Urban Dilemma.* Toronto: McClelland and Stewart Limited, 1972.

Elliot, Jean Leonard. *Minority Canadians -- Native Peoples.* Scarborough, Ont.: Prentice-Hall of Canada Ltd., 1972.

Frideres, J.S. *Canada's Indians -- Contemporary Conflicts.* Scarborough, Ont.: Prentice-Hall of Canada Ltd., 1974.

Knight, Rolf. *Indians at Work,* Vancouver: New Star Books, 1978.

Knox, R.H. and Nicholson, J. Philip. *Indian Conditions -- A Survey.* Ottawa: Department of Indian Affairs and Northern Development, 1980.

Krotz, Larry. *Urban Indians -- The Strangers in Canada's Cities.* Edmonton: Hurtig Publishers Limited, 1980.

La Roque, Emma. *Defeathering the Indian.* Agincourt, Ont.: The Book Society of Canada, 1975.

Littlejohn, Kathy and Powell, Rick. *A Study of Native Integration into the Fort McMurray Labour Force.* Unpublished document prepared for the Alberta Oil Sands Environmental Research Program by the Canadian Institute for Research in the Behavioural and Social Sciences, 1980.

Nagler, Mark. *Indians in the City -- A Study of the Urbanization of Indians in Toronto.* Ottawa: Saint Paul University, Canadian Research Centre for Anthropology, 1973.

Nagler, Mark. *Natives Without a Home.* Don Mills, Ont.: Longman Canada Limited, 1975.

Neils, Elaine M. *Reservation to City, Indian Migration and Federal Relocation.* Chicago: University of Chicago, Department of Geography, 1971.

Paton, Richard. "Summary of Urban Indians and Native Studies." Policy Division, Policy, Research and Evaluation Branch, Department of Indian Affairs and Northern Development, 1977.

Ponting, J. and Gibbins, R. *Out of Irrelevance.* Toronto: Butterworth and Co. (Canada) Ltd.

Robertson, Heather. Reservations Are For Indians. Toronto: James Lorimer & Company, 1970.

Ryan, Joan. *Wall of Words -- The Betrayal of the Urban Indian.* Edmonton: Peter Martin Associates Limited, 1978.

Steiner, Stan. *The New Indians.* New York: Dell Publishing Company Inc., 1968.

Stymeist, David H.   *Ethnics and Indians -- Social Relations in a Northwestern Ontario Town.* Edmonton: Peter Martin Associates Limited, 1977.

Van Dyke, Edward W., with special assistance from Carlene A. Van Dyke. *Lives in Transition: The Ft. Mackay Case.* Prepared for the Office of the Northeast Alberta Regional Commission by Applied Research Associates Ltd., Ponoka, Alberta, 1978.

Waddell, Jack O. and Watson, O. Michael, eds. The American Indian in Urban Society.   Toronto: Little, Brown & Company (Canada) Limited, 1971.

Walsh, Gerald. *Indians in Transition.* Toronto: McLelland and Stewart Limited, 1971.

Weaver, Sally. Making Canadian Indian Policy: The Hidden Agenda 1968–1970. Toronto: University of Toronto Press, 1981.

Institute Management

The Institute for Research on Public Policy

Publications Available*
June 1983

Books

Leroy O. Stone & Claude Marceau	*Canadian Population Trends and Public Policy Through the 1980s*. 1977 $4.00
Raymond Breton	*The Canadian Condition: A Guide to Research in Public Policy*. 1977 $2.95
Raymond Breton	*Une orientation de la recherche politique dans le contexte canadien*. 1977 $2.95
J.W. Rowley & W.T. Stanbury, eds.	*Competition Policy in Canada: Stage II, Bill C-13*. 1978 $12.95
C.F. Smart & W.T. Stanbury, eds.	*Studies on Crisis Management*. 1978 $9.95
W.T. Stanbury, ed.	*Studies on Regulation in Canada*. 1978 $9.95
David K. Foot, ed.	*Public Employment and Compensation in Canada: Myths and Realities*. 1978 $10.95
W.E. Cundiff & Mado Reid, eds.	*Issues in Canadian/U.S. Transborder Computer Date Flows*. 1979 $6.50
David K. Foot, ed.	*Public Employment in Canada: Statistical Series*. 1979 $15.00
Meyer W. Bucovetsky, ed.	*Studies in Public Employment and Compensation in Canada*. 1979 $14.95
Richard French & André Béliveau	*The RCMP and the Management of National Security*. 1979 $6.95
Richard French & André Béliveau	*La GRC et la gestion de la sécurité nationale*. 1979 $6.95
Leroy O. Stone & Michael J. MacLean	*Future Income Prospects for Canada's Senior Citizens*. 1979 $7.95

---

* Order Address: The Institute for Research on Public Policy
P.O. Box 9300, Station A
TORONTO, Ontario
M5W 2C7

Richard M. Bird — *The Growth of Public Employment in Canada*. 1979 $12.95

G. Bruce Doern & Allan M. Maslove, eds. — *The Public Evaluation of Government Spending*. 1979 $10.95

Richard Price, ed. — *The Spirit of the Alberta Indian Treaties*. 1979 $8.95

Richard J. Schultz — *Federalism and the Regulatory Process*. 1979 $1.50

Richard J. Schultz — *Le fédéralisme et le processus de réglementation*. 1979 $1.50

Lionel D. Feldman & Katherine A. Graham — *Bargaining for Cities. Municipalities and Intergovernmental Relations: An Assessment*. 1979 $10.95

Maximo Halty-Carrere — *Technological Development Strategies for Developing Countries: A Review for Policy Makers*. 1979 $12.95

G.B. Reschenthaler — *Occupational Health and Safety in Canada: The Economics and Three Case Studies*. 1979 $5.00

David R. Protheroe — *Imports and Politics: Trade Decision Making in Canada, 1968–1979*. 1980 $8.95

G. Bruce Doern — *Government Intervention in the Canadian Nuclear Industry*. 1980 $8.95

G. Bruce Doern & Robert W. Morrison, eds. — *Canadian Nuclear Policies*. 1980 $14.95

Allan M. Maslove & Gene Swimmer — *Wage Controls in Canada: 1975–78: A Study of Public Decision Making*. 1980 $11.95

T. Gregory Kane — *Consumers and the Regulators: Intervention in the Federal Regulatory Process*. 1980 $10.95

Albert Breton & Anthony Scott — *The Design of Federations*. 1980 $6.95

A.R. Bailey & D.G. Hull — *The Way Out: A More Revenue-Dependent Public Sector and How It Might Revitalize the Process of Governing*. 1980 $6.95

Rejean Lachapelle &
Jacques Henripin

*La situation démolinguistique au Canada :
évolution passée et prospective.* 1980 $24.95

Raymond Breton,
Jeffrey G. Reitz &
Victor F. Valentine

Cultural Boundaries and the Cohesion of Canada.
1980 $18.95

David R. Harvey

*Christmas Turkey or Prairie Vulture? An Economic
Analysis of the Crow's Nest Pass Grain Rates.*
1980 $10.95

Richard M. Bird

Taxing Corporations. 1980 $6.95

Leroy O. Stone &
Susan Fletcher

A Profile of Canada's Older Population. 1980
$7.95

Peter N. Nemetz, ed.

Resource Policy: International Perspectives.
1980 $18.95

Keith A.J. Hay, ed.

*Canadian Perspectives on Economic Relations With
Japan.* 1980 $18.95

Raymond Breton &
Gail Grant

*La langue de travail au Québec : synthèse de la
recherche sur la rencontre de deux langues.*
1981 $10.95

Diane Vanasse

L'évolution de la population scolaire du Québec.
1981 $12.95

Raymond Breton,
Jeffrey G. Reitz &
Victor F. Valentine

Les frontières culturelles et la cohésion du Canada.
1981 $18.95

H.V. Kroeker, ed.

Sovereign People or Sovereign Governments.
1981 $12.95

Peter Aucoin, ed.

*The Politics and Management of Restraint in
Government.* 1981 $17.95

David M. Cameron, ed.

*Regionalism and Supranationalism: Challenges
and Alternatives to the Nation-State in Canada and
Europe.* 1981 $9.95

Heather Menzies

*Women and the Chip: Case Studies of the Effects of
Informatics on Employment in Canada.*
1981 $6.95

Nicole S. Morgan

*Nowhere to Go? Possible Consequences of the
Demographic Imbalance in Decision-Making
Groups of the Federal Public Service.* 1981 $8.95

Nicole S. Morgan   *Où aller? Les conséquences prévisibles des déséquilibres démographiques chez les groupes de décision de la fonction publique fédérale.* 1981 $8.95

Peter N. Nemetz, ed.   *Energy Crisis: Policy Response.* 1981 $18.95

Allan Tupper &   *Public Corporations and Public Policy in Canada.* G. Bruce Doern, eds.   1981 $16.95

James Gillies   *Where Business Fails.* 1981 $9.95

Réjean Lachapelle &   *The Demolinguistic Situation in Canada: Past* Jacques Henripin   *Trends and Future Prospects.* 1982 $24.95

Ian McAllister   *Regional Development and the European Community: A Canadian Perspective.* 1982 $13.95

Robert J. Buchan,   *Telecommunications Regulation and the* C. Christopher Johnston,   *Constitution.* 1982 $18.95 T. Gregory Kane, Barry Lesser, Richard J. Schultz & W.T. Stanbury

W.T. Stanbury &   *Regulatory Reform in Canada.* 1982 $7.95 Fred Thompson

Rodney de C. Grey   *United States Trade Policy Legislation: A Canadian View.* 1982 $7.95

John Quinn &   *Non-Tariff Barriers After the Tokyo Round.* Philip Slayton, eds.   1982 $17.95

R. Brian Woodrow &   *The Introduction of Pay-TV in Canada: Issues and* Kenneth B. Woodside, eds.   *Implications.* 1982 $14.95

Stanley M. Beck &   *Canada and the New Constitution: The Unfinished* Ivan Bernier, eds.   *Agenda.* 2 vols. 1982 $10.95

Douglas D. Purvis, ed.,   *The Canadian Balance of Payments: Perspectives* assisted by Frances Chambers   *and Policy Issues.* 1983 $24.95

Roy A. Matthews   *Canada and the "Little Dragons."* 1983 $11.95

Charles Pearson &   *Trade, Employment, and Adjustment.* 1983 $5.00 Gerry Salembier

Charles F. Doran	*Economic Interdependence, Autonomy, and Canadian/American Relations.* 1983 $5.00
F.R. Flatters & R.G. Lipsey	*Common Ground for the Canadian Common Market.* 1983 $5.00
E.P. Weeks & L. Mazany	*The Future of the Atlantic Fisheries.* 1983 $5.00
Steven Globerman	*Cultural Regulation in Canada.* 1983 $11.95

Occasional Papers

Raymond Breton & Gail Grant Akian (No. 5)	*Urban Institutions and People of Indian Ancestry: Suggestions for Research.* 1979 $3.00
K.A.J. Hay (No. 6)	*Friends or Acquaintances? Canada and Japan's Other Trading Partners in the Early 1980s.* 1979 $3.00
Thomas H. Atkinson (No. 7)	*Trends in Life Satisfaction Among Canadians, 1968–1977.* 1979 $3.00
Fred Thompson & W.T. Stanbury (No. 9)	*The Political Economy of Interest Groups in the Legislative Process in Canada.* 1979 $3.00
Pierre Sormany (No. 11)	*Les micro-esclaves : vers une bio-industrie canadienne.* 1979 $3.00
Zavis P. Zeman & David Hoffman, eds. (No. 13)	*The Dynamics of the Technological Leadership of the World.* 1980 $3.00
Russell Wilkins (No. 13a)	*Health States in Canada, 1926–1976.* 1980 $3.00
Russell Wilkins (No. 13b)	*L'état de santé au Canada, 1926–1976.* 1980 $3.00
P. Pergler (No. 14)	*The Automated Citizen: Social and Political Impact of Interactive Broadcasting.* 1980 $4.95
Donald G. Cartwright (No. 16)	*Official Language Populations in Canada: Patterns and Contacts.* 1980 $4.95

Reports